THE PENGUIN MAHABHARATA

Bishnupada Chakravarty was born in 1947. He is the author of several books on religion, science and children's literature in Bengali.

Debjani Banerjee holds a PhD in Postcolonial Literature and Cultural Studies, and does translation work for the Kolkata-based Mono Translation Bureau.

Also available in this series

The Penguin Companion to the *Ramayana*

The Penguin Companion
to the
Mahabharata

Original text by
Bishnupada Chakravarty

Translated from the Bengali by
Debjani Banerjee

PENGUIN BOOKS

PENGUIN BOOKS

Published by the Penguin Group

Penguin Books India Pvt. Ltd, 11 Community Centre, Panchsheel Park, New Delhi 110017, India

Penguin Group (USA) Inc., 375 Hudson Street, New York, NY 10014, USA

Penguin Group (Canada), 90 Eglinton Avenue East, Suite 700, Toronto, Ontario, M4P 2Y3, Canada (a division of Pearson Penguin Canada Inc.)

Penguin Books Ltd, 80 Strand, London WC2R 0RL, England

Penguin Ireland, 25 St Stephen's Green, Dublin 2, Ireland (a division of Penguin Books Ltd)

Penguin Group (Australia), 250 Camberwell Road, Camberwell, Victoria 3124, Australia (a division of Pearson Australia Group Pty Ltd)

Penguin Group (NZ), cnr Airborne and Rosedale Roads, Albany, Auckland 1310, New Zealand (a division of Pearson New Zealand Ltd)

Penguin Group (South Africa) (Pty) Ltd, 24 Sturdee Avenue, Rosebank, Johannesburg 2196, South Africa

Penguin Books Ltd, Registered Offices: 80 Strand, London WC2R 0RL, England

First published in Bengali by Ananda Publishers Pvt. Ltd 1998
First published in English by Penguin Books India 2007
This translation copyright © Penguin Books India 2007

ISBN 10: 0-14310-208-7   ISBN 13: 978-0-14310-208-3

Typeset in ITC Stone by InoSoft Systems, Noida
Printed at Thomson Press, Noida

Cover painting depicts Gita sermon—Krishna removing Arjuna's reluctance to fight against kinsmen, based on the *Mahabharata*, Kangra, Pahari, circa AD 1800–10.
Courtesy by the National Museum

Contents

About the *Mahabharata*

The *Mahabharata* is called the fifth Veda. Of all the epics ever composed, the *Mahabharata* is the longest and, without doubt, the greatest.

Scholars are not unanimous about the date of composition of the *Mahabharata*. According to some, Vyasdeva wrote it in 3000 BC. Others think it was composed before that.

The *Mahabharata* is divided into the following eighteen episodes:

1. Adi Parva (The First Episode)
2. Sabha Parva (The Assembly Episode)
3. Aranyaka Parva; also, Vana Parva or Aranya Parva (The Forest Episode)
4. Virata Parva (In the Land of Virata)
5. Udyoga Parva (Getting Ready)
6. Bhishma Parva (The Bhishma Episode)
7. Drona Parva (The Episode of Drona)
8. Karna Parva (The Episode of Karna)
9. Shalya Parva (The Episode of Shalya)
10. Sauptika Parva (The Episode of the Night Battle)
11. Stri Parva (The Episode of the Wives)
12. Shanti Parva (The Episode of Peace)
13. Anushasana Parva (The Episode of Instructions)
14. Ashwamedhika Parva (The Ashwamedha Episode)
15. Ashramavasika Parva (Living in the Ashram)
16. Mausala Parva (The Episode of the Mallet)
17. Mahaprasthanika Parva (The Final Journey)
18. Svargarohana Parva (Ascent to Heaven)

The Story of the *Mahabharata*

Adi Parva

Vashishtha curses the Ashtavasus

Vashishtha's wish-cow Kamdhenu was not to be found. The Ashtavasus had stolen the cow and hidden her. The Ashtavasus were the eight sons of Vasu, the daughter of King Daksha. The sage Vashishtha was furious and cursed them, saying, 'You will be born on earth.'

What a calamity! We have to be born on earth! The Ashtavasus ran to Ganga, saying, 'Mother, help us!'

'Oh my dears, do not worry!' Ganga assuaged their fears. 'I will take birth as your mother. As soon as you are born I will throw you into my waters and you can return to heaven. You will not have to spend much time on earth.'

Shantanu marries Ganga

One day, Shantanu, son of Pratip, the king of Hastinapur, was walking along the banks of the river Ganga. Suddenly, he saw a beautiful young woman rising out of the waters of the Ganga. 'Is this a goddess or an apsara? Such beauty, such youth! I must have her!'

'Who are you, goddess? Will you marry me?' Shantanu's voice was pleading, his eyes were beseeching.

'It is a great honour to be the life partner of the great king Shantanu; but I have two conditions, o king.'

'I am willing to comply with all your conditions.' Shantanu was beside himself with emotion.

'The first condition is that you will never want to know who I am. The second condition is that you will never question my actions. If you break your word I will disappear.'

'As you wish. Come, my goddess, take refuge in my embrace. I am willing to give up my life for you,' Shantanu beseeched.

Bhishma is born

One after another, Ganga sacrificed seven children into the waters of the Ganga. Thunderstruck, Shantanu bore all this in silence as he was afraid of breaking his word.

But with the eighth child, the barriers of his patience broke. 'Stop! Who are you? You must tell me the reason for your cruelty and madness.'

As Ganga revealed all, Shantanu calmed down. Ganga said, 'I am taking this boy with me. He will come back to you in good time. He was the main culprit who stole Nandini so he will have to stay longer on earth. In his previous birth, he was the eighth Vasu.'

As she had promised, Ganga returned the boy when he was thirty-six years old to Shantanu. She had taught him all he needed to know to become the ideal king. He was called Devavrata. Shantanu celebrated the coronation of Devavrata as the crown prince.

Satyavati

Earlier it was Ganga; this time it was Yamuna.

Satyavati, the daughter of the king of fishermen, King Dasa, was crossing the ferry on the river Yamuna. She glowed with beauty. Shantanu was infatuated again by beauty.

King Dasa said, 'If you marry Satyavati, her son must become king.'

'No! No! I will not hear of it. This is impossible! But Satyavati? How will I live without her?' Troubled, Shantanu gave up food and sleep.

Bhishma makes a difficult promise

When he heard what had happened, Devavrata rushed to King Dasa. 'Please save my father.' he said. 'I promise that Mother Satyavati's son will be king.'

King Dasa said, 'You can withdraw your claim to the throne; but what about your sons? What certainty is there that they will give up their claims to the throne?'

'I promise that I will not marry. I will remain single all my life.'

The gods, sages and apsaras showered flowers on Devavrata. This was a difficult, or bheeshan, promise; hence his name became Bhishma.

'What a sacrifice for one's father!' Shantanu said. 'I give you a boon; you will die only when you want to die.'

Shantanu got Satyavati. He had two sons by her, Chitrangad and Vichitravirya. Shantanu died before his sons grew up.

Vichitravirya becomes king

Bhishma, who was supposed to have worn the crown himself, placed, ironically, the royal crown on Vichitravirya's head.

Chitrangad died an untimely death, killed by a gandharva king, also called Chitrangad. Vichitravirya was too young, so Bhishma began to look after the royal affairs as his guardian. When he became an adult, Vichitravirya became king.

Amba, Ambika, Ambalika

When it was time for the king to get married, elder brother Bhishma forceably picked up the three beautiful daughters of the king of Kashi—Amba, Ambika and Ambalika—from their own swayamvar gathering. His objective was to marry his brother to the three girls.

But Amba had other plans. She had wanted to marry the king of Shalva, but when she saw Bhishma, she expressed her love to him.

Bhishma was shocked. 'This is an impossible proposition. I have vowed to be single forever.' he said.

Spurned, Amba cursed Bhishma, 'You are pushing me to my death. Well, I curse you that I shall be the cause of your death in your next life.'

Amba sacrificed herself to fire. In her next life she would be reborn as Shikhandi and would cause Bhishma's death, although his death was coveted by him as per the blessings of his father.

Vichitravirya indulged in worldly pleasures with his two wives. Like his brother Chitrangad, he died at a young age without any heirs.

Dhritarashtra, Pandu and Vidura

How would the dynasty continue? At Satyavati's request, her illegitimate son Vyasdeva fathered Dhritarashtra by Ambika, Pandu by Ambalika, and Vidura by a servant woman.

Dhritarashtra was born blind, so he could not become king. Pandu became king. His complexion was pale; thus he was called Pandu, meaning pale.

Vidura was greatly committed to justice. He always gave the right advice and spoke up against justice. He was also very virtuous.

Dhritarashtra was married to Gandhari, the daughter of Subal, the king of Gandhar. Gandhari's sacrifice was unrivalled; because her husband was blind, she blindfolded herself. She was also very scholarly.

The Pandavas and Kauravas are born

Vyasdeva had given a boon to Gandhari, 'May you be the mother of a hundred sons.'

Gandhari gave birth to a hundred sons and one daughter. The sons were named Duryodhana, Dushasana, etc., and the daughter was named Dushala.

When Gandhari was pregnant, a maid, Saubali, looked after

Dhritarashtra.

Dhritarashtra had a son, Jujutsu, by Saubali. Jujutsu joined hands with the Pandavas during the Kurukshetra war and was the only one of Dhritarashtra's sons to survive the war.

Pandu married Kunti, the adopted daughter of the king of Kuntibhoj, and Madri, the sister of King Shalya of Madra.

By the curse of a sage, Pandu was unable to beget children. At Pandu's request, Kunti and Madri invoked the gods to impregnate them. Dharma, Pavan, Indra and the two Aswini kumaras responded to their call.

When Kunti was still unmarried, to test her own powers she had invoked Surya. Karna, fathered by Surya, was born to Kunti. Kunti put Karna in a basket and floated him down the river. Adhirath, a charioteer, saw the newborn baby and brought him home. He and his wife Radha reared Karna with love and care, like their own son. They named him Vasusena.

The ninth ancestor of Dhritarashtra and Pandu was Kuru, the founder of the Kaurava dynasty. By that measure, they and their successors were all Kauravas. But only Dhritarashtra's sons were called Kauravas. Pandu's sons were called Pandavas. The land that was blessed by Kuru's meditation was known as Kurukshetra (kshetra means place).

Yudhishthira was the oldest amongst the Kauravas and Pandavas. Bheema and Duryodhana were born on the same day.

Pandu died an untimely death. Dhritarashtra looked after the Pandavas with as much affection as he had for as his own sons.

The beginning of the hostilities

No one could match Bheema's strength. The Kauravas were annoyed by his attacks and mischievousness. To take revenge, they poisoned Bheema's food and fed it to him. When he fell unconscious, they threw him into the water. Bheema rolled until he reached the underworld.

The other Pandavas were not aware of the Kauravas' conspiracy. They looked for Bheema.

In the underworld, Bheema was bitten by snakes. Poison acted as an antidote to poison; after eight days, Bheema regained consciousness.

Vasuki, the king of serpents, was a close friend of Bheema's maternal grandfather, Kuntibhoj. He made Bheema drink amrit, the nectar of life. Having drunk amrit, Bheema's strength increased a hundredfold.

With invincible strength, Bheema came back to his mother and brothers. He recounted the entire episode. Yudhishthira said, 'The

Kauravas are our brothers. Their disgrace is ours. So do not mention this incident to anybody.'

Dronacharya arrives

The princes were playing with a wooden ball. It fell into a well. They tried to pull it out but could not. The princes hung their heads in shame; this was the extent of their learning!

A Brahmin was passing by. His countenance inspired respect. When he discovered what had happened he said, 'Oh that is the problem, is it? Here, I'll throw my ring into the well; now watch how both your ball and my ring are retrieved.'

The Brahmin cut off a blade of grass and its sharp edge pierced the ball. He threw another blade of grass and then another, each blade of grass piercing the one in front of it. Thus he made an unbroken chain with the grass and easily pulled the ball up. The boys' eyes opened wide in surprise. They were very happy to have their ball back.

Then the Brahmin shot an arrow which pierced the ring and retrieved it. The princes, beside themselves with joy, informed Bhishma.

When Bhishma heard these stories he guessed that the newcomer was none other than Dronacharya; no one else had these powers. He went himself to meet Drona and appoint him to train the princes in the use of arms. So far the princes had been learning from Kripacharya. Now they would have a great teacher.

Drona thought, 'This is for the best. These princes will be able to teach Dhrupad a lesson. They will be able to avenge my insult.'

When they were learning the use of weapons from the great ascetic Agnivesh, Dhrupad had promised Drona that when he became king, he would share his kingdom with his friend, Drona.

Many days passed. When Drona's son Ashwathama clamoured for milk, the rich boys diluted a paste of pounded rice with water and gave it to him. Thinking that he was drinking milk, Ashwathama jumped with joy. The rich boys clapped and jeered at him.

Drona watched this happen. He was deeply hurt. He recalled his friend's promise and rushed to him.

But much greater humiliation awaited Drona there. Dhrupad said, 'Friendship is amongst equals. There is no question of a friendship between a prosperous king and a poor Brahmin.'

Drona came to Hastinapur to avenge this insult.

By Drona's training, the princes became skilled warriors. But Arjuna surpassed them all. Drona said, 'Arjuna! I will train you such that you will have no rival in the three worlds.'

At Duryodhana's request, Drona also taught Karna. Karna was to become Arjuna's main rival.

Ekalavya

The prince of hunters requested Drona to teach him but his request was rejected.

One day the princes went hunting for deer. A loyal dog accompanied them.

As soon as the dog entered the forest he began barking. After a while the dog, silenced, returned. A skilled archer had shot seven arrows so that the dog could not bark; he was not bleeding but the arrows had sealed his jaws together.

The princes were astonished. To satisfy their curiosity, they went into the heart of the forest and saw a forester practising archery in front of Drona's statue. He had matted hair and was wearing the skin of a black deer. It was Ekalavya!

The princes returned. Annoyed, Arjun asked Drona, 'Did you not say that there would be no one as skilled as me in archery in the three worlds? But I do not have the skill that Ekalavya has!'

Drona came to Ekalavya. Ekalavya paid his respects to him and said, 'Order your disciple, my teacher.'

Drona said, 'Cut off the thumb of your right hand and give it to me.' Ekalavya carried out this cruel order with an impassive face.

Drona was relieved, as was Arjuna. Ekalavya had sacrificed his excellence to clear the way for his teacher's favourite disciple, Arjuna, to establish his brilliance.

Drona tests the princes

To test the concentration of his students, Drona placed an artificial bird on the branch of a tree and asked the princes to string arrows on to their bows. He asked everybody the same question, 'What can you see?'

Everyone answered, 'We can see trees, the bird, the sky and other things.'

Drona was annoyed. At the very end, Arjuna said, 'I can only see the head of the bird.'

Drona was heartened. He said, 'Shoot the arrow.' Arjuna's arrow sliced off the head of the bird.

Drona said, 'You will be able to teach Dhrupad a lesson.'

One day a crocodile caught Drona. He could have freed himself, but to test his students, he screamed, 'Save me, save me.' Everyone was helpless, except Arjuna who saved his teacher by shooting arrow after arrow, demonstrating great prowess.

Drona was pleased and gave Arjuna a great weapon called Brahmasira. He said, 'Do not use this weapon unless it is absolutely necessary.'

The princes display their skills

One day, the princes, with Drona's encouragement, displayed the skills they had acquired. The spectators praised them profusely. When Bheema and Duryodhana were on the brink of a real fight, Ashwathama dissuaded them. Arjuna created fire by the fire arrow, water by the water arrow and wind by the wind arrow and thus proved his excellence.

Then Karna, with Drona's permission, displayed all the skills that Arjuna had. Karna and Arjuna were locked in a battle. When they were about to fight, Kripacharya intervened. He said, 'Karna, Arjuna is the son of Pandu and Kunti. He is born in the Kuru dynasty. You cannot fight with him unless we know who your parents are and what dynasty you belong to.'

Karna bowed his head in shame. How would he introduce himself?

Immediately, Duryodhana crowned Karna the king of Anga.

Bheema said, 'The son of a charioteer cannot be involved in equal combat with Arjuna, just as a dog can never get food that is offered in sacred rituals.'

Karna looked at his progenitor, Surya, his face reddened in humiliation.

During the course of this argument, the sun had set. The archery display came to an end. Everyone was relieved but the hostilities between the Pandavas and the Kauravas could not be kept secret any longer.

Dhrupad is taught a lesson

In accordance with Drona's advice, the princes attacked the kingdom of Panchal. Dhrupad was defeated, mainly because of Arjuna's bravery. Drona told Dhrupad, 'You did not keep your promise but I will. I am returning half the kingdom to you so that our friendship is between equals.'

Yudhishthira becomes crown prince

A year later, Dhritarashtra nominated Yudhishthira the crown prince. Duryodhana was blind with envy and anger. On the advice of his uncle Shakuni, he convinced Dhritarashtra that he ask the Pandavas and Kunti to go to Varanavat for a few days.

Yatugriha

The aged Dhritarashtra, unwilling but blinded by filial love, sent the Pandavas and Kunti to Varanavat. Duryodhana had already sent a trusted mason, Purochan, to Varanavat. He had constructed a house with wax, flax, oil, wood and other inflammable materials; if it were touched by an ember it would go up in flames and the Pandavas and their mother would be killed. The path to Duryodhana's coronation would be free of thorns.

Vidura sent a trusted digger who dug a huge tunnel for the Pandavas to escape.

Bheema set fire to the house of wax and escaped through the tunnel.

A hunter's wife was sleeping inside with her five sons. Seeing their charred bodies, all those concerned believed, gleefully, that Kunti and her five sons had been burnt to death.

Dhritarashtra shed a few crocodile tears. Along with Bhishma and the Kauravas, he offered prayers for the Pandavas in the river Ganga.

Hirimba

The Pandavas, tired and thirsty, sat under a large banyan tree. Bheema heard the cries of a stork and said, 'There must be water nearby. I will fetch some, while you rest.'

Bheema used his clothes to carry water. He saw that everyone was sleeping so he chose not to disturb them.

The ferocious monster Hirimb lived in that forest. He smelled human beings and sent his sister Hirimba to catch them.

On seeing Bheema, Hirimba was mesmerized. Upon her delay, Hirimb rushed to the forest; Bheema threw him to the ground and killed him.

On the advice of his mother, Bheema married Hirimba. Hirimba gave birth to a son named Ghatotkach.

Bak rakshasha

The wanderings of the Pandavas led them to the village of Ekchakra. They took shelter in the house of a Brahmin.

Bak, a wicked monster, lived in the village. Every day one man from the village would carry a large portion of rice and buffalo meat for him and Bak would eat the food and the man.

Then, it was the turn of the man who had given shelter to the Pandavas. His family shed copious tears. Kunti assured them, 'Don't worry. Today Bheema will go, he will kill Bak.'

Bheema went to Bak and started eating Bak's food in front of him. Bak's blows and kicks did not interrupt Bheema's eating. After eating to his heart's content, Bheema turned his attention to Bak. He threw him to the ground and crushed him to death.

Hearing Bak's screams, the monsters came rushing. Bheema roared, 'I am warning you! If you ever eat humans again, I will kill all of you.' The monsters said, 'Yes sir! We promise never to do such things again.'

Draupadi

After being humiliated by Drona, Dhrupad arranged for a yagna, a sacrificial offering. He wanted to have a son who would kill Drona and avenge this insult.

From the holy smoke of the yagna, a lustrous boy, Dhristadyumna, was created. He did eventually kill Drona, although by dishonest means.

A lustrous girl was also born of the fire; her complexion was dusky and she was beautiful. No one could avert his eyes from her. And why should they? The goddess Lakshmi had been reborn as King Dhrupad's daughter. But that's another story.

The girl had many names; as Dhrupad's daughter she was Draupadi. She was dusky and thus was called Krishna (krishna means dark). She emanated from the fire of a sacred ritual or yagna and thus she was called Yagnaseni. She was the princess of Panchal and therefore she was called Panchali.

The Pandavas heard of Draupadi's swayamvar when they were in Ekchakra. They left for Panchal immediately. On their way, Arjuna defeated the gandharva Chitrarath. From Chitrarath, Arjuna learned the art of visualizing; like present-day television, it helped Arjuna see what was happening in the three worlds.

In Panchal, the Pandavas took shelter with a potter. As in Ekchakra, they begged in the guise of Brahmins.

At the swayamvar, many powerful kings were present as were ascetics and gandharvas. Lord Krishna himself was present, along with Balarama.

The Pandavas came in their disguise. Seeing Lord Krishna and Balarama, they paid their respects, silently, in their hearts.

Krishna saw the disguised Brahmins, bright as embers and covered with ash, and whispered to Balarama, 'Do you recognize the Pandavas? I knew they were not burnt in that house of wax.'

When Dhristadyumna entered with the bride Draupadi, there arose a murmur, so captivated was everybody by her beauty.

Dhristadyumna said, 'This is my sister, Draupadi. The target is above us. Below is a mechanical, circular path. Whoever can shoot an arrow through the path and hit the target can have my sister as his bride, whatever his caste or creed.'

One by one, great warriors came to try their luck. They were all knocked out and returned disgraced. Karna came forward but before he could aim for the target Draupadi said that she would not be willing to marry the son of a charioteer.

Karna tried to hide his anger under a crooked smile. But can anger be suppressed? His entire body convulsed with rage. He looked at his father Surya and controlled himself as he returned to his seat.

The kings had their turns. Everyone was defeated and insulted. One Brahmin got up. Some said, 'What is wrong with this Brahmin? But fools rush in where angels fear to tread.'

Others said, 'He is no fool. He will be able to do this. See, he is so well built, almost as tall as a tree. His arms are long enough to touch his knees. His chest is as expansive as a huge field. His eyes are like lotuses. And what determination shines in them! What confidence! He moves with the proud gait of a lion and yet he is still as the Himalayas. Patient! He will be able to do it.'

Arjuna asked Dhristadyumna, 'I hope your sister has no objections to marrying a Brahmin?'

'Objections? I have been waiting for you, the Lord of my heart! You may not be aware of this. But I know! And the omniscient Lord Krishna knows. Please accept me and make my life worth living,' Draupadi said silently.

Seeing Arjuna, Krishna was restless.

Dhristadyumna said, 'No! She has no objections.' In his heart, Arjuna thought of Mahadeva and Krishna and effortlessly shot at the target.

There were celebrations in court. The gods showered blessings from heaven. Drums were beaten. Songs hailing Arjuna's achievements were sung.

And Draupadi? She was almost unconscious with joy and excitement. She walked towards Arjuna, slowly, with trembling feet. The veils of abashment almost slipped off. She garlanded Arjuna, and unblinkingly looked at him. In her heart, she paid her respects to Lord Krishna. Who knew whether days of happiness had begun for her, or days of unending misery?

Meanwhile, the defeated kings attacked Dhrupad when they saw that a Brahmin was taking Draupadi away. Arjuna rushed to protect Dhrupad with his bow and arrow. Bheema vanquished the kings by attacking them with trunks of huge trees.

Kunti, on the other hand, was worried. 'It's been a while since my sons went to beg for food. It's so late and they have not come home.'

Then she heard, 'Mother, see what alms we have brought for you today.'

Wasn't that Yudhishthira's voice?

'Share what you have brought between yourselves!' Kunti said from inside the house.

A mother's command must be heeded. So Draupadi married all five brothers.

'Who is there? O friend Krishna! Balarama! How did you come here?' Arjuna asked.

In reply to Arjuna's question, Krishna said, 'We recognized you.' To Yudhishthira he said, 'Fire cannot ever be suppressed by ashes. Even so, you should remain in disguise a little longer.'

Dhrupad learnt of the true identity of his sons-in-law. He was overwhelmed with joy. He had wished for sons-in-law exactly like them.

Returning home

The news soon spread. Vidura rushed to give Dhritarashtra the good news.

Dhritarashtra was full of remorse at the incident of Yatugriha. As soon as he heard the news, he said, 'Vidura, you must bring them back right away. Let Draupadi be welcomed with the honour she deserves. The palace must be filled with festivities.'

Duryodhana and Karna wanted to kill their enemies without further delay. They tried to poison Dhritarashtra. Bhishma, Drona and Vidura advised the king to divide the kingdom. That would ensure the happiness of all.

In accordance with Krishna's advice, the Pandavas returned. The people of Hastinapur wished them long lives and took part in joyous celebrations.

Khandavprastha

By Dhritarashtra's orders, the kingdom was divided; the Pandavas went to Khandavprastha or Indraprastha and the Kauravas remained in Hastinapur.

With time, Khandavprastha began to look like a beautiful, impressive city. Yudhishthira was very concerned about the welfare of his subjects; Saraswati and Lakshmi, learning and wealth, prospered in his kingdom. The people were very happy.

Arjuna is banished to the forest

'Thief! Thief! He is running away with my cows!' a helpless Brahmin cried for help.

'Don't worry! I will bring my weapon immediately.' Arjuna assured him.

Arjuna entered the armoury to get his weapon, not knowing what was in store for him; Yudhishthira and Draupadi were in the armoury. According to the initial condition, when one brother was in a room with Draupadi, none of the other brothers could enter the room. The punishment for breaking this rule was steep—twelve years in the forest.

Arjuna helped the Brahmin retrieve his cow and then went to beg forgiveness from Yudhishthira. He said, 'Brother, give me permission. I must go to the forest.'

Yudhishthira tried to rationalize with Arjuna. But Arjuna's resolve was firm. 'I will go to the forest,' he said and he went.

Draupadi fainted. Arjuna was indeed unparalleled. Who could be compared to him? How would Draupadi spend twelve years without him?

Kidnapping Subhadra

Arjuna was roaming forests and holy places. Meanwhile two princesses, Ulupi, the daughter of the god of serpents, and Chitrangada, the daughter of the king of Manipur, had given their hearts to him. In Pravas, he met his great friend Krishna. They had much to talk about and celebrate. The Yadavas were having a festival on the Raibatak Parbat. Balarama was wandering about with his associates.

Arjuna was restless. 'Krishna, who is that beauty?' he asked.

Krishna understood his friend. 'Do you like her? Fine, you may kidnap her. She is my sister Subhadra.'

Arjuna came in a fast chariot and kidnapped Subhadra. He turned the chariot towards Indraprastha. Balarama was agitated, but Krishna placated him. Then he accompanied Arjuna.

Setting fire to Khandava

'Having had ghee continuously for twelve years, I have lost my taste. Now I must have a lot of meat to regain my taste. I am trying to burn Khandava forest and devour it but I am unable to do so. Indra's friend Takshak dwells here; as soon as I set fire to the forest, Indra brings rain clouds and the rain puts out the fire. Can you two help me in this regard?' Agni, dressed as a Brahmin, asked Krishna and Arjuna.

Krishna and Arjuna were travelling towards Indraprastha with Subhadra. They said, 'We can try if we get the right weapons.'

Agni gave Arjuna the Gandeev bow, an inexhaustible quiver, and the Kapidhwaj chariot. He gave Krishna a Sudarshan chakra and a club called Koumodoki.

Agni happily roasted the animals in the fire and ate them. Krishna and Arjuna guarded the forest with their weapons so that no animal could escape.

Takshak was not in the forest. Apart from him, only six animals, Takshak's son Ashwasena, the giant Moy and four birds escaped alive.

Krishna and Arjuna's bravery pleased Indra and he gave his godson Arjuna many weapons. He gave Krishna a boon, 'Your friendship with Arjuna will be forever.'

Sabha Parva

The Giant Moy Builds an Assembly Hall

'You have saved my life. Tell me, what can I do for you?' the giant Moy, with folded hands, asked Arjuna.

Arjuna said, 'Do something for my friend; that will make me happy enough.'

Krishna said, 'Build such a palace for Yudhishthira that no one in the three worlds would ever have seen one like it.'

Moy brought precious gems from the Mainak mountain. He brought a club for Bheema and a god-gifted conch shell for Arjuna. A magnificent palace was built. Jewels and marble were used inside it to build ponds, gardens, fish, fruit and flowers. It was an elaborate affair.

The Pandavas moved in on an auspicious day. The story of this assembly hall spread far and wide. Kings and saints from distant lands came and lived in this hall with the Pandavas.

Killing Jarasandha

Narad visited Yudhishthira's splendid hall and said, 'Yudhishthira, you must perform the Rajasuya Yagna. I met Pandu in heaven; he is also of the same opinion.'

The Pandavas did not do anything without consulting Krishna. Krishna said, 'That is an excellent suggestion; however, defeating King Jarasandha of Magadha is a problem. His general Sisupala is invincible. Jarasandha has imprisoned eighty-six kings. When he has arrested one hundred kings he will sacrifice them all to the altar of the god Rudra. Balarama and I have left Mathura and are now residing in Dwarka because we are afraid of Jarasandha. First and foremost, Jarasandha needs to be killed.'

Yudhishthira said, 'Peace is more important than happiness. There is no need for the Rajasuya Yagna.'

Bheema and Arjuna, instead of supporting their brother, began to arrange for the killing of Jarasandha. Krishna also wanted Jarasandha to be killed; that is what happened.

Krishna, Bheema and Arjuna disguised themselves as Brahmins and went to meet Jarasandha. Jarasandha was about to wash the feet of the Brahmins when Krishna revealed their true identities. He said, 'Either you release the kings you have imprisoned, or you can choose one amongst us who will send you to your death.'

Rather than releasing the prisoners, Jarasandha chose Bheema.

The fight lasted thirteen days. On the fourteenth day, Bheema pulled Jarasandha by his legs and tore him apart. Jarasandha was killed.

When Jarasandha was born, the right and left halves of his body were born separately. A female rakshasha Jara had pieced the two sides together and thus he was called Jarasandha. Krishna had told Bheema about this and so it had been easier for Bheema to kill Jarasandha.

Bheema and Arjuna released all the kings who had been imprisoned. Krishna asked them to be present at Yudhishthira's Rajasuya Yagna.

Next, Yudhishthira concentrated on the royal coffers. Arjuna went north, to the wealthy Kuber, Bheema went east, Nakula, west, and Sahadeva went south. Much wealth was deposited in the royal treasury.

The Rajasuya Yagna

Yudhishthira began to make preparations for the Rajasuya Yagna on the advice of the royal priest Dhoumya. Kings and sages from all over the world visited. Bhishma, Dhritarashtra, Vidura and all the Kauravas attended. The yagna began amidst much pomp and grandeur.

Yudhishthira delegated the work. Bhishma and Drona were the chief advisors, Dushasana was in charge of food, Ashwathama was in charge of looking after the Brahmins, Sanjay was in charge of looking after the kings. Kripacharya was responsible for looking after the treasury and bestowing charity. Vidura was appointed the treasurer. Duryodhana was in charge of accepting gifts and Krishna was going to wash the feet of the Brahmins.

The yagna over, Bhishma called Yudhishthira and said, 'Give gifts to people here according to their status. Give a special gift to the greatest of all the people gathered here.'

Yudhishthira asked, 'Who is that special person?'

Bhishma said, 'Why, Krishna, of course. There is none here who can equal him.'

As soon as Sahadeva, by Yudhishthira's order, handed the special gift to Krishna, Sisupala became angry and maligned Krishna profusely.

Bheema was about to teach Sisupala a lesson. Bhishma stopped him.

Bhishma said, 'Let him go. He will jump into the fire like an insect and burn himself to death.' He told Sisupala, 'You are criticizing Krishna. Why don't you fight him instead?'

Krishna smiled and said, 'I had promised the mother of this worthless person that I would forgive a hundred follies committed by him. Today his wrongdoings have exceeded a hundred. Therefore...' Saying this, Krishna, using the Sudarshan chakra, beheaded Sisupala.

While returning to Dwarka, Krishna told Yudhishthira, 'Just as animals look towards clouds and birds look upon trees as their refuge, may the Brahmins in your kingdom look upon you as their shelter. Look after your subjects with sincerity.'

Duryodhana burns with envy

Duryodhana and the Kauravas stayed for a few more days at the palace constructed by the giant Moy. Duryodhana was humiliated at every step. He mistook clear marble for water and lifted his clothes to walk through the water. Then he mistook water for dry land and got his clothes wet. The marble doorway was so clear that he walked into it. Another time, he mistook an open doorway for a wall and kept looking for an exit. Everyone laughed at him. He returned to Hastinapur, burning with shame, humiliation and hatred. Envy and the inability to bear others' prosperity almost drove him to suicide.

When his cunning maternal-uncle Shakuni heard this, he said, 'Don't worry, Duryodhana. Listen to me calmly. Tell your father to invite Yudhishthira to a game of dice. Yudhishthira is addicted to dice; he will definitely come. Leave the rest to me.'

At first, Dhritarashtra did not agree. But when Duryodhana scared him with threats of killing himself, he relented. Vidura repeatedly objected but Dhritarashtra's good sense had, by then, been overshadowed by his blind love for his son.

To pacify Duryodhana, Dhritarashtra ordered the construction of a luxurious palace in Hastinapur, along the lines of the palace built by the giant Moy. It was decided that the game of dice would be held here.

Vidura came and told Yudhishthira of all that had transpired. Yudhishthira did not want to be a part of this petty scheme. However, thinking that if he did not go his uncle may feel insulted, he finally set off for Hastinapur with Draupadi and his four brothers.

Yudhishthira loses in the dangerous game of dice

'Playing dice with bets is indeed vile. It is a sin; there is no valour in it, nor is there any greatness.' Yudhishthira said to Shakuni but, provoked by him, began to play. This was the beginning of a new chapter in the suffering of the Pandavas.

Shakuni played on behalf of Duryodhana.

Yudhishthira was defeated every time by Shakuni's chicanery. Initially, Yudhishthira had bet an expensive necklace; his second bet was a box of a hundred coins. His third bet was hundreds of dressed-up maids. Then he started wagering on all his wealth; finally he even bet on his brothers. Then he bet upon himself. Finally, he wagered his beloved queen Draupadi.

Duryodhana, Dushasana and Shakuni were beside themselves with joy. Vidura advised Dhritarashtra to give up Duryodhana as the black sheep of the family; as a result he was insulted by Duryodhana. Bhishma and Drona and the other adults watched the proceedings helplessly. When they won Draupadi, the Kauravas jumped with joy.

The disrobing of Draupadi

The wicked Duryodhana haughtily ordered Vidura, 'Go, get Draupadi.' he said. 'She has to sweep the floors of our houses.'

Vidura said, 'Oh, you fool! You don't seem to understand how low you stoop. A deer must not provoke a tiger! Don't worry, you will surely be destroyed.'

Duryodhana, the beast, was drowning in fiendish pleasure. By Duryodhana's orders, a charioteer went to bring Draupadi. He entered Draupadi's room fearfully.

The mighty Draupadi gave a menacing cry; 'Go to the assembly and find out whom Yudhishthira wagered first, himself or me. Only if he wagered me first, will I go. Otherwise I will not.'

When Duryodhana heard the charioteer's message, he was mad as an injured lion. He told Dushasana, 'Go, pull her by her hair and bring her here.'

Dushasana pulled Draupadi by her hair and brought her to the assembly. Much slander and torture was unleashed upon her.

Draupadi shook with anger and hatred. She said, 'Shame on this court! Have all values evaporated? Are Bhishma, Drona and all the other wise men dead? A royal court that does not have any wise men is not a court. Those who do not stand up for what is right are not wise. That which does not contain truth cannot be right. And that which is filled with trickery is not the truth.'

The words of the powerful and wise Draupadi made the elders at the court hang their heads in shame. Another person protested. He was Vikarna, Duryodhana's brother. He said, 'This is wrong, this is against all principles. Just because King Yudhishthira behaved irresponsibly, it is wrong to humiliate a helpless woman who has done no wrong; this is a grave sin.'

Dushasana pulled at Draupadi's clothes in order to disrobe her. Draupadi, with all her heart, began to invoke her guru, Krishna. 'O Madhusudan, o Janardan, o Krishna! Please ward off my shame!'

Once, in her previous life, Draupadi had torn off a piece of her cloth and given it to a holy man to cover his body; when the holy man had gone to the river to have a bath, his loin cloth had been washed away. The holy man had blessed Draupadi, saying, 'If you are ever in a similar situation, the lord Srihari will help you hide your shame.'

Dushasana could not finish pulling Draupadi's robes which, by Krishna's illusory powers, had become limitless. The more he pulled, the more the cloth extended; from a distant point, Krishna was supplying more and more cloth.

Duryodhana pulled up his clothes from his thigh and signalled to Draupadi to sit on it.

Bheema jumped forward with a torch. He said, 'I will burn the hand, stained with sin, with which my older brother Yudhishthira played the game of dice.'

Arjuna restrained Bheema. Bheema promised, 'I will tear the flesh from the chest of that brute Dushasana and drink his blood. I will break the thigh of that fiendish Duryodhana with my club and smash it into a thousand pieces.'

Jackals and donkeys began to make sounds that boded ill. Fearful of some great evil that would befall them, everyone began to invoke peace. The elders present explained to Dhritarashtra that he should save the Pandavas in this time of danger; otherwise, the destruction of the Kauravas would be inevitable. Such terrible wrongs would not go unpunished.

It was as if Dhritarashtra had regained his consciousness. He castigated himself. 'Shame on me!' he said. 'How did I tolerate this for so long? Not just tolerate, I even enjoyed it! Again and again I asked, "Did we win?" Shame!'

Dhritarashtra sent for Draupadi. He embraced her affectionately and said, 'Dear, please forget what has ensued. Let me repent for the sins that I have committed. Ask for three boons from me.'

Draupadi used the three boons to get back herself, her husbands and all their wealth.

Dhritarashtra expressed his apologies to Yudhishthira. The Pandavas returned to Indraprastha.

The dangerous game of dice

But no! The Pandavas did not make it back to Indraprastha. On the way, they met a messenger who said that another game of dice had been arranged. Dhritarashtra had called for them.

The wicked foursome, Duryodhana, Dushasana, Karna and Shakuni were, of course, responsible. They thought, 'Oh no! What has Dhritarashtra done! All our plans and conspiracies have come to naught. Does an injured snake ever let go of one who has wounded it? It becomes even more vicious and waits for an opportunity to take revenge. So, let the Pandavas return. We will play again. If they lose this time they have to go to the forest for thirteen years. During the last year they will have to live in disguise. By that time, surely these thorns in our flesh can be taken care of.'

Dhritarashtra, born blind, was doubly blinded by his love for his sons. Although his wife Gandhari reproached him and warned of impending disaster, Dhritarashtra bowed to the unreasonable demand of his son.

Yudhishthira heard the messenger through and said, 'Whatever God wishes will happen. Let us go back.'

Again the honest Yudhishthira was tricked into defeat by the crafty Shakuni in a game of dice. Although it was this defeat that paved the way for the victory of the Pandavas and brought for the Kauravas the punishment they deserved, who knew then what fate had in store for them?

Setting off for the forest

Draupadi and the five Pandavas cast aside their royal robes and wore deerskin. They came to take leave of their elders including Bhishma, Drona, Dhritarashtra and Vidura. The elders hung their heads in shame; no one said a word. Their eyes misted.

Only Vidura said, 'Right will invariably triumph over wrong.' He did not let Kunti go to the forest. She stayed back with him.

But Kunti? How could Kunti, who had borne such wonderful children, stay away from her sons and her daughter-in-law? Kunti, in tears, broke down. She was joined by Gandhari and all the other daughters-in-law of the Kaurava dynasty.

Draupadi and the five Pandavas set off for the forest leaving everyone devastated. This was also exactly what had happened when Rama, Lakshmana and Sita had gone to the forest.

The people of the kingdom criticized the Kauravas and prayed to God for the well-being of the Pandavas.

Dushasana trailed after Bheema, mocking him and calling him a cow.

Bheema said, 'Just wait, Dushasana. I will tear your chest apart and drink your blood.'

In response to Karna's mockery Arjuna said, 'Karna, know this, that if I do not kill you on my return, the Himalayas will be dislodged. The sun will lose its lustre and the moon will not be cool any longer.'

Sahadeva said, 'You depraved Shakuni; I will only find peace when I kill you.'

The priest Dhoumya and hundreds of Brahmins and citizens accompanied the Pandavas. They said, 'We will not stay in this hell a moment longer.'

As desired by Dhritarashtra, Vidura gave a running commentary on the journey of the Pandavas.

There was thunder in a clear sky. The earth trembled. There was a solar eclipse and the sun disappeared behind the moon. Meteors crashed. The united cries of vultures, crows and foxes boded ill.

Aranyaka Parva

The Pandavas begin staying in the forest

The Pandavas walked northwards. They spent their first night in the forest under a banyan tree on the banks of the river Ganga. Yudhishthira requested the Brahmins to return. The Pandavas could subsist on meat but what would the Brahmins eat? The Brahmins did not want to return.

Yudhishthira prayed to Surya. Surya was pleased and gave him a plate. He said, 'For as long as Draupadi does not finish eating, the rice in this plate will not finish. This will happen everyday.' Thus, miraculously, the problem was solved.

Kirmit, the brother of Bak rakshasha, lived in that forest. To avenge his brother's death, he attacked Bheema, but Bheema killed him.

Krishna came to meet them. He, ostensibly, did not know about the game of dice. Who then had prevented Draupadi from being disrobed?

Dwaitavan, on the banks of the river Saraswati, had a lot of fruit. An ashram was built there. The Pandavas, along with Draupadi, began to live there.

The conversation between Yudhishthira and Draupadi

(Time: Evening; Place: The riverside; People present: Yudhishthira, Bheema, Draupadi)

Draupadi: I feel really sorry to see you in this state.

Yudhishthira: Why?

Draupadi: What a sorry state the five Pandavas are in today! Could this not have been avoided? Kshatriyas should be forgiving when required and valorous when required. If that day we had shown our valour, would we have to stay in this forest wearing deerskin, today?

Yudhishthira: Beloved, I do accept that sometimes anger does help us derive superficial benefits. But anger causes destruction. Can a valorous person be an angry person as well? He who is truly valorous does not lose his sense of judgment even when angry.

Draupadi: Morality protects those who protect morality. It is the duty of a king to protect morality and you are doing that sincerely. But where are morals, in turn, protecting you?

Yudhishthira: If one adheres to moral principles in the hope of a profit then one is engaging in a commercial transaction. I have to do my duty, whether I benefit from it or not. That is my principle.

Draupadi: I accept that. But one who leaves everything to fate is bound to suffer. A lazy person can never earn money. The farmer has to depend on rain for his agriculture but he has to plough the land as well. Similarly, for good or bad results one has to depend on the Lord but one has to use one's strength to go on trying. Only then will the Lord's blessings be showered upon us.

Bheema: Draupadi is right, o king! The duty of a Kshatriya is to use his power to restrain evil. It is the duty of a sage to live in the forest and eat fruit.

Yudhishthira: I accept that I was wrong. But it was not my decision to come to the forest. My mistake was in agreeing to play the game of dice and that too with wagers; to honour my promise I had to come to the forest. It is my principle to honour my promise.

A battle between Mahadeva and Arjuna

Vyasdeva taught Yudhishthira the art of Pratismriti. Yudhishthira taught it to Arjuna who used it to pray to Indra. Indra said to him, 'Pray to Mahadeva.'

At the end of Arjuna's severe penance, Mahadeva appeared in the guise of a hunter. A battle ensued over who had killed a wild boar. Finally, Mahadeva revealed his true form and gave Arjuna the weapon Pashupat. Indra, Varuna, Kuber and Yama also gave him many kinds of weapons. Indra sent his charioteer Matli and Arjuna was brought to heaven in a divine chariot. He kept his godson with him for five years and taught him various kinds of weaponry. From the gandharva Chitrasena, Arjuna learned dance and music, including playing instruments.

From one shrine to another

The sage Lomesh came from heaven, carrying with him the news that Arjuna was in heaven and was fine. Yudhishthira and the others were relieved.

From Dwaita forest, Draupadi and the four Pandavas went on a pilgrimage. They travelled to Gomti, Prayag, Gaya, Agastya ashram, Vrigutirtha, Mahendra mountain, the south, Pravas, Gandhamadan mountain, Vadrika ashram and many other holy places.

Bheema meets Hanuman

Draupadi saw a beautiful lotus with a hundred petals at Vadrika ashram. She told Bheema, 'I want many lotuses like that.'

Bheema set out to get the lotuses. On the way he met Hanuman who assured him that he would help the Pandavas in every way possible. When Bheema was about to pluck the flowers from Kuber's garden, there was an altercation between him and Kuber's soldiers; however, Draupadi and the other Pandavas reached the spot before the situation worsened. Kuber organized a comfortable stay for them at Gandhamadan.

Nahush, who was cursed, was about to kill Bheema when Yudhishthira answered the complex spiritual questions of the python and caused Bheema to be released.

Meanwhile, Arjuna killed three million giants who were enemies of Indra and returned to his brothers.

Duryodhana is put in his place

'You have many cows in Dwaita forest. Why don't we go there under the pretence of seeing the cows? How can we be satisfied unless we witness with our own eyes the misery of the Pandavas and Draupadi?' the cunning Shakuni advised the wicked Duryodhana.

The gandharva Chitrasena was then roaming about, for his pleasure, in Dwaita forest. Duryodhana became entangled in a battle with Chitrasena over the construction of a playhouse. Chitrasena easily beat the Kauravas to a pulp and imprisoned them.

Duryodhana's ministers came rushing to Yudhishthira, 'Save us, o king! The Kauravas are in great danger.'

Bheema jumped up in happiness and said, 'Great! Chitrasena, this is what is required. Beat up those fellows.'

By Yudhishthira's orders, the Pandavas went and released Duryodhana with his queen, Dushasana, Karna and Shakuni.

Durvasa is dealt with

The sage Durvasa came to Duryodhana's palace with ten thousand disciples. The evil Duryodhana, with folded hands, said to Durvasa, 'Kindly visit the Pandavas with your disciples in the afternoon when Draupadi has finished eating.'

Draupadi had finished her meal. Durvasa reached with his ten thousand disciples. He said, 'We will take a dip in the river and be right back. But once we are back we want food immediately. We are all extremely hungry. If I do not get food, I will burn everything to ashes.'

'O Krishna! Save me, o Lord! O Madhusudan! O Lord who looks after his devotees! There is no more food on my plate. What am I to do now! You find a way for those who have no hope!' Draupadi, in great distress, prayed.

God always rushes to help his troubled devotees. Krishna appeared before Draupadi and said, 'Bring your plate. Is there not a morsel of food on it?'

Draupadi brought her plate. 'There it is; there is a bit of rice on the plate. I am eating this morsel of rice. My satisfaction will bring satisfaction to all. I am full. Go and see, Durvasa and his disciples must be satiated as well. I am leaving now. When you are in trouble you must pray to Madhusudan.'

When Sahadeva went to call them, he saw that the sage Durvasa and his group had escaped. Becoming suddenly over-full scared them.

The Pandavas ate venison every day. One day the deer in the forest told Yudhishthira, 'O Lord! If you stay any longer in this forest our families will perish. Please save us.'

Yudhishthira left Dwaita forest and moved to Kamyak forest.

Draupadi is abducted

One day, Duryodhana's sister Dushala's husband Jayadratha, the king of Sindhu, came to meet Draupadi. He came stealthily, like a thief, when the Pandavas had gone deer-hunting. Draupadi was alone. He forced Draupadi on to his chariot and escaped with her.

As soon as Yudhishthira learnt what had happened he sent off Bheema and Arjuna. Bheema used the half-moon arrow to scalp

Jayadratha's hair. He would have beheaded him but he did not have Yudhishthira's permission.

'Jayadratha is Mother Gandhari's son-in-law. Our only sister will be widowed. Let it be, Bheema,' Yudhishthira said.

Jayadratha, thoroughly insulted, prayed to Shiva in the Himalayas and was given the boon that except Arjuna, he would be able to defeat all the Pandavas in a one-day battle.

Karna gives his armour and earrings to Indra

Karna was born with divine earrings and impenetrable armour. He was invincible.

Indra knew this. He, however, was a great friend of the Pandavas; he was also Arjuna's biological father. So he thought of a ploy to get the armour and earrings from Karna.

Karna was famous for his charitable nature. Every day, after his bath, he would pray to his father Surya. At that time if a Brahmin asked for something he never refused.

Indra grabbed the opportunity. In the guise of a Brahmin, he asked Karna for his armour and earrings. Even though Karna knew that giving these away would make his death inevitable, Karna did not hesitate. Indra, surprised and overwhelmed, blessed Karna; he also gave him the weapon Shakti that never missed its mark.

Yudhishthira and the crane have a conversation

The Pandavas came from Kamyak forest to Dwaita forest again.

One day, a Brahmin came and complained, 'O great king! A deer has run away with two pieces of wood, Arani and Mantha, on its antlers. The pieces of wood were part of my yagna. Can you please retrieve them for me; otherwise the yagna will be marred.'

Yudhishthira and his brothers went out to look for the deer but could find nothing. They became tired and thirsty. Nakula climbed up on a tree and said, 'Perhaps there is a body of water in the distance; I can hear the sounds of water-birds.'

Yudhishthira said, 'Go and fetch water for all of us in your quiver. Don't be late.'

The water in the pond was clear as crystal. 'O let me drink to my heart's content.' Nakula cupped his hands to drink the water.

'Don't drink water without answering my question.'

'Who speaks? I can't see anyone anywhere. Forget it! Let me quench my thirst and then I'll find out who was speaking.'

As soon as Nakula drank the water, he died.

When he didn't return, Yudhishthira sent Sahadeva in search of his brother. Then, when Sahadeva didn't return, Arjuna was sent and then Bheema. Eventually Yudhishthira set out himself to find the dead bodies of his brothers lying next to the pond.

Crane: I am a bird called a crane. If you try to drink water without answering my question you too will be in this state.

Yudhishthira: I am sure that you are not a mere bird. Whoever you are, ask me your question.

Crane: What is heavier than earth?

Yudhishthira: Mother.

Crane: Who is located higher than the sky?

Yudhishthira: Father.

Crane: What travels faster than the wind?

Yudhishthira: The mind.

Crane: What grows faster than grass?

Yudhishthira: Worries.

Crane: Who is the biggest enemy?

Yudhishthira: Anger.

Crane: Which disease can never be cured?

Yudhishthira: Greed.

Crane: Who is a saint?

Yudhishthira: One who looks after the wellbeing of all creatures.

Crane: Who is a sinner?

Yudhishthira: One who is cruel.

The crane volleyed many such questions. Yudhishthira answered all of them.

Crane: I am not a bird. I am Dharma and I have come to test you. I am very happy to hear your answers. I will rejuvenate one of your brothers; tell me whom do you want back?

Yudhishthira: I want Nakula back.

Crane: Why did you want your stepbrother Nakula rather than your brave brothers Bheema and Arjuna?

Yudhishthira: Every one of my brothers is special to me. But I thought that as I, one of Mother Kunti's sons, am alive; one of Mother Madri's sons should be alive as well.

Crane: Bravo Yudhishthira! You really are great. Your sense of justice is unparalleled. I am returning the life of all your four brothers. I want to grant you two boons.

Yudhishthira: Please return the logs of wood that the Brahmin was using for his yagna so that he can complete his yagna.

Crane: Hear! Hear! Yudhishthira. Here are the pieces of wood. What is the second boon?

Yudhishthira: May we not be recognized during the year in which we need to stay in disguise.

Crane: Granted!

Virata Parva

The Pandavas come in disguise to Viratanagar

The Pandavas came to Viratanagar, the capital of Matsya country, to spend their one year of living in disguise. At the entrance of the city was an acacia tree. They hung all their weapons in a bundle on the branch of that tree. They also hung a corpse from that branch. The stench would prevent people from venturing that way. No one would suspect that there were weapons there. One cannot be overcautious, they thought.

King Virata was holding court. A handsome, well-built Brahmin came in. It was Yudhishthira.

King Virata: Oh Brahmin! Who are you?

Yudhishthira: I am Kanka, a friend of Yudhishthira. I can play dice very well. If you keep me in the royal court you will be happy.

Virata: Oh excellent! You may stay in my court.

The next day Bheema came in the guise of a cook carrying ladles and spuds. He said, 'I am Vallabh! I can make excellent dishes.' At once, he was appointed as the royal chef.

Then Draupadi came. She said, 'I am Sairindhri! I have five gandharvas as my husbands. I am skilled at dressing hair, making garlands, painting pictures and scattering fragrances.'

'You are not only skilful, you are beautiful as well. Come with me to the inner sanctum of the house,' said Queen Sudeshna.

Arjuna came into the court with his long plaited hair swaying behind him. 'I am Vrihannala. I want to teach music and dance to the princess. I have learned music and dance at a higher level.' He was thus appointed to teach dance and music to Princess Uttara.

Sahadeva, taking the name of Aristanemi, was appointed as the vet to look after the cattle in the royal cattle-yard.

Nakula said, 'I am an expert on horses. My name is Granthik.' The king gave him the responsibility of looking after his stables.

Killing Keechak

Keechak was the king's brother-in-law, the brother of Queen Sudeshna. Although he was a wayward character, he had tremendous influence in the royal family. He noticed Draupadi and his demeanour towards her turned ugly.

Draupadi kept Bheema informed of everything. Bheema said, 'Ask him to come to the theatre house tonight. Tell him that you will wait for him there. I will take care of him once and for all.

Keechak, beside himself with joy, came stealthily to the theatre house in the middle of the night. Bheema was lying there, covered with a sheet.

Mistaking him for Draupadi, Keechak touched him. Bheema caught hold of him by the throat and killed him. Everyone assumed that Sairindhri's gandharva husbands had killed Keechak.

Duryodhana tries to steal cows and is outwitted

Duryodhana got news from his spies that there was no news of the Pandavas. Perhaps they were dead. Keechak, the brother-in-law and general of King Virata was also dead. Susharma, the king of Trigarta, said, 'The king of Virata has grown too big for his boots. Let us take this opportunity and rob his cows and his wealth.' Duryodhana agreed happily.

Susharma went ahead and attacked the kingdom of Matsya. He was followed by Duryodhana's army. They stole many cows and Susharma took King Virata as his prisoner.

Yudhishthira felt that they could not be inactive any longer. One must protect he who has given one shelter. By Yudhishthira's directions Bheema went to save Virata. He uprooted a large tree.

'Bheema, no! If you do that people will recognize you as Bheema. Just use a plain bow and arrow to fight.'

Bheema did exactly that. Susharma was imprisoned and Virata was released. Yudhishthira ordered the release of Susharma.

King Virata and the four Pandavas (except Arjuna) were busy resisting Susharma in the south-east. Meanwhile, Duryodhana attacked from the north-west. Bhishma and Drona were also there. They stole sixty thousand cows from Virata. The person in charge of cows brought the news to Prince Uttar.

Uttar was just a boy and was also alone. He said, 'If I had a suitable chariot and charioteer I would show Duryodhana.'

Vrihannala said, 'Where is the worry? I will be your charioteer.'

Uttar said, 'But you are a woman! How will you drive a chariot?'

Vrihannala stubbornly insisted until Uttar agreed. But when he went to the battlefield and saw the huge Kaurava army, young Uttar was frightened. He said, 'Oh please, do turn the chariot around. Otherwise I will jump.' Saying this, he jumped out of the chariot.

Arjuna caught hold of Uttar and said, 'If you are so scared, you drive the chariot. I will fight. First let us go to the acacia tree at the entrance of the kingdom and get our weapons.'

'Weapons, tree? I cannot comprehend anything.' Uttar said.

'Have you heard of Arjuna?'

'Arjuna, the best archer in the three worlds? Who has not heard of him?'

'I am Arjuna. Kanka is Yudhishthira. Vallabh is Bheema. Granthik is Nakula. Aristanemi is Sahadeva. And Sairindhri is our wife Draupadi.'

Uttar was speechless with joy and surprise. Arjuna cast aside his feminine attire. He strung the bow.

When Drona heard the sound of the stringing of a bow, he realized that it must be Arjuna. 'But thirteen years have not elapsed. If they were caught, they would have to go to the forest for another twelve years. Would Arjuna take that risk?'

The astrologer counted and said, 'Thirteen years have passed, o king!'

Duryodhana shrieked.

Six arrows came and pierced the ground near Drona's feet. Another six grazed his ears. His favourite disciple had bowed to him and asked after his wellbeing. Drona was beside himself with joy.

All the cows were rescued. Duryodhana and his party were defeated.

As for the Pandavas, their lives were saved but what about honour? King Virata was delighted to find out the true identity of the Pandavas. Arjuna and Subhadra's son Abhimanyu was married to Uttara.

Udyoga Parva

Krishna is visited by Duryodhana and Arjuna

Krishna said, 'You Pandavas have gone through a lot. Now you must prepare to win back the kingdom you have lost.' Saying this, Krishna returned to Dwarka.

Balarama said 'Let a messenger of peace be sent to the Kauravas; it is best to come to a mutual settlement.'

Satyaki said, 'Settlement will not be enough. We want war.'

The messenger of peace went to Hastinapur. According to Dhrupad's advice, envoys were also sent to various countries to ask for help in the event of war.

Arjuna went to Dwarka. Duryodhana arrived there on the same day. Krishna was taking a nap. Arjuna sat at his feet and Duryodhana near his head.

When he opened his eyes Krishna saw Arjuna first. He said, 'On the one hand is me, on the other is my army comprising of hundreds and thousands of Narayani soldiers. You can choose one of the two. One thing—in the war I may act as a charioteer but I will not handle weapons. When I opened my eyes I saw Arjuna first; further, Arjuna is younger; so, Arjuna, you choose first.'

Arjuna said, 'Friend, you know that if I have you I do not want anything else in this world.'

Duryodhana thought, 'Arjuna is rather a fool, is he not? What will Krishna do alone? Then again he says he is not going to use weapons. Anyway, I have managed to get what I wanted. So what is my worry?'

No kingdom without war

The kings were divided down the middle. Satyaki, Dhristaketu, Dhrupad and Virata came on the side of the Pandavas. Their total number of soldiers was huge, consisting of foot soldiers, cavalrymen, fighters on elephant-back and charioteers.

Bhagadatta, Shalya, Kritavarma, Jayadratha and Sudakshin were on the side of the Kauravas. Their army was even larger.

Yudhishthira sent a message through an envoy saying that the Kauravas should return their kingdom. If they did not agree to that they could write five villages in the names of the five brothers. They would be happy with that as peace was greater than prosperity.

Bhishma, Drona and even Dhritarashtra wanted peace.

But Duryodhana and Karna wanted war. The conceited Duryodhana said arrogantly, 'I will not give any land, not even that which sticks on the edge of the needle, without war.'

The aged Dhritarashtra wiped away his tears and said, 'What can mere mortals do against that which fate has ordained? What will happen is inevitable.'

Krishna fails as a messenger of peace

Krishna said, 'Let me make one last effort and see if I can persuade Duryodhana to change his mind. But first let me know your opinions.'

Except Sahadeva and Draupadi everyone wanted to avoid war. None of them wanted to kill his own relative. Sahadeva said, 'There must be a war. Only then will they learn a lesson.'

'When you bring the message of peace to the court of the Kauravas, do not forget, Krishna, that the depraved Dushasana pulled me by my hair in front of everybody and brought me to the court. He abused me in the vilest language. He tried to disrobe me. If you had not protected my dignity, think of my plight today. I do not know anything beyond you, O Lord. But you must do what you think is best.' Draupadi said, crying piteously.

Krishna came to Hastinapur but could not change Duryodhana's belligerent attitude. He said to Gandhari, 'Mother! Please talk to your son.'

But fair words cannot butter a parsnip. War seemed inevitable.

Conversation between Karna and Krishna

Krishna was returning home having failed in his mission. 'Oh, isn't that Karna? Yes, indeed it is. Let me speak to him and see.'

'Karna! Perhaps you do not know that you are the eldest Pandava. You are Kunti's eldest son.'

Karna hung his head. He sighed, 'I know Krishna but it is too late. I am bound by my promise to Duryodhana. I cannot go back on my word.'

Conversation between Kunti and Karna

'Karna!'

'Who is that? Oh! Mother Kunti! Why have you come here and that too alone?' Karna touched his mother's feet with great respect.

'Karna, one day when I was immature, I committed a mistake. I have to pay for it as long as I live. Come my dear, come home with me.'

'No mother! I cannot do that. It is too late. Forget about Karna, mother! But when you, my mother, have come to my door, I give you my word, that other than Arjuna I will not kill any of your sons. Either Arjuna or I, one of us will survive; you will have five sons, either way.'

The sounds of horns, drums and trumpets

The seven groups of the Pandava army were headed by Dhrupad, Virata, Dhristadyumna, Shikhandi, Satyaki, Chekitan and Bheema. The main general was Dhristadyumna and Arjuna was the chief commander.

Duryodhana made Kripa, Drona, Shalya, Jayadratha, Sudakshin, Kritavarma, Ashwathama, Bhurisraba, Shakuni, Vahlik generals of each division of the army. Bhishma disliked Karna. So he said that he would not take up arms if Karna did. Karna had similar reservations. For the time being, Karna remained away from the main action. Bhishma was the commander-in-chief.

Vyasdeva granted divine sight to Sanjay so that he could watch the battle from inside the palace and describe it for Dhritarashtra. Was this a precursor to live satellite television? The sounds of horns, drums and trumpets could be heard. Innumerable conch shells were blown.

Bhishma Parva

The rules of battle

The two sides got together and agreed upon some rules of battle.

One—There would be fighting only during the day; at sunset, fighting would stop. Then there would be mutual amity.

Two—There would be fighting only between equals. A foot soldier would fight a foot soldier, a cavalryman would fight a cavalryman, and so on.

Three—One who stood aside from the battle will not be attacked.

Four—One cannot attack somebody who was unarmed and without an armour.

Five—Charioteers, flag bearers, people who were giving the weapons or nursing the wounded could not be attacked.

Eventually, not all these rules were obeyed scrupulously. There was lack of commitment on both sides.

The dialogue between Krishna and Arjuna:
Srimadbhagawad Gita

'Krishna, steer the chariot to a place between where the Pandavas and the Kauravas stand. Let me see the people I have to fight against,' said Arjuna.

Krishna brought the chariot between the two warring parties. Arjuna looked carefully around him. Then, in a voice drenched with emotion, he said, 'Krishna! This is impossible. I cannot be part of this war. My body is trembling. The bow seems to fall out of my grip.'

'Friend, why is this happening to you?' Krishna wanted to know.

'Grandfather Bhishma, my teacher Dronacharya, Kripacharya and my brothers are in front of me. I have to get our kingdom back by killing them? Leave aside kingdom, I don't even want to go to heaven by killing them. I don't need to go to war. I will become a mendicant and beg, even that is better; but I cannot kill them.' Arjuna broke down.

Krishna became sombre. He said, 'You are the best amongst the brave. If this is what you have to say how do you think the others will react? Don't think like a coward. Let the man within you be awakened.'

'But, Krishna, I don't see this war bringing anything other than the destruction of families, of religion and ill-will.'

'Arjuna, do not forget that you are a Kshatriya. If you do not fight against evil, you are not doing your duty. And you are talking about killing your own relatives? Please know that their deaths have already been decided. No one can lift a finger outside of my wishes. And the soul is indestructible. Death is a function of the body. The soul has no birth and no death. Just as human beings get rid of their old clothes and wear new clothes, the soul goes from one body to another according to the consequences of one's own actions or karma. So do not grieve.'

'I understand all of that, Krishna, but...'

'Even then you say but? Even now you have doubts? All right then, see my real form.'

'What is this? Krishna! What is this? The entire world is entering your body—rivers, mountains, forests, everything! The sun and the moon are like your two eyes. What is this I behold? Today, my life has been worth living; I have spoken as a friend to you.

'I may have done much wrong without knowing it. Krishna, forgive me. I am your servant. Please order me; tell me what I have to do.'

'You have risen like a brave soldier! Now, look ahead. Decide on your duty. Do not forget that your duty is the most important moral principle. And if you can do that in a detached way then you can earn my proximity. Oh Bharat! Whenever moral principles are stained by immorality and evil raises its ugly head, then, in order to save the good and virtuous, to destroy sinners and to re-instate religion to its rightful place of glory, I am born again and again, in every yuga. I am an avatar in every yuga.'

Yudhishthira gets his blessings

Yudhishthira touched Bhishma's feet and sought his blessings. Bhishma said, 'I am dependant on them for my daily livelihood. So I have to take up weapons in their favour. But remember, victory will be theirs who have followed the right path.' Drona and Kripa said similar things. In response to Yudhishthira's call, Yuyutsu, Duryodhana's stepbrother came over to join the Pandavas.

The battle began. Kurukshetra, a religious place, was transformed into a large battlefield.

Bhishma alone was like a hundred warriors. Countless warriors lost their lives to him. He killed ten thousand soldiers every day and thus in nine days he alone killed ninety thousand soldiers.

Yudhishthira realized the graveness of the situation. He thought that if Bhishma continued to fight in this way they would have no soldiers left. On the ninth night he went and discussed his fears with Bhishma.

Bhishma said, 'Don't worry, keep Dhrupad's son Shikhandi in front and carry on your battle. In his previous birth he was Amba. When I see her I will not take up arms any more, then you can kill me.'

The next day, keeping Shikhandi ahead, Arjuna attacked Bhishma with a volley of arrows. Before sunset his body pierced with arrows fell to the ground. But there were so many arrows in his body that the body did not touch the ground; he lay on a bed of arrows.

The Pandavas left their weapons and rushed to see their grandfather. The Kauravas came as well.

Bhishma said, 'Can you get me a pillow?' Duryodhana ran and got him a soft downy pillow.

But Bhishma was not satisfied. He said, 'No, this pillow does not become a Kshatriya. Arjuna.'

Arjuna understood what his grandfather wanted. With three arrows Arjuna provided a pillow for Bhishma's head. Despite so much pain, Bhishma's face was lit by a smile.

Arjuna had spent so much time lying on Bhishma's lap and asking questions; it broke his heart to have to make a pillow with arrows for him. Tears trickled down his face.

The next morning everyone came to visit Bhishma. He said, 'I am really thirsty.' Duryodhana brought cold water. Bhishma said, 'No, not this water. Send for Arjuna.'

Arjuna drew out, with one arrow, cool water from the earth. Bhishma blessed Arjuna profusely. Then he called Duryodhana and said, 'There is still time. Call truce with the Pandavas, otherwise destruction is inevitable.'

But the wicked do not listen to sane advice. Duryodhana did not pay any heed to Bhishma's words.

'I am Karna, the one you despise.' Karna came and stood next to Bhishma.

'Shame on you Karna! I used to rebuke you because you gave bad advice to Duryodhana. Do you know that you are the eldest brother of the Pandavas? Will you fight against your brothers now?'

'What can I do? I have promised Duryodhana.'

'Alright then; fight for the right path at least and then you can go to heaven.' Karna paid his respects to Bhishma and, wiping his tears, went away.

Drona Parva

Arjuna is saved by Krishna

On the eleventh day Karna became the general of the Kauravas. He tried to take Yudhishthira as his prisoner but Arjuna did not let that happen.

On the twelfth day, Arjuna was kept busy by Susharma, the king of Trigarta. Bheema attacked Drona. Bhagadatta aimed the weapon Vaishnava at Arjuna. Krishna came forward and took it on his chest; the weapon became a garland in his neck. If Krishna had not done this, Arjuna would definitely have been killed.

Killing Abhimanyu

'You are being partial towards the Pandavas, that is why we are unable to win,' Duryodhana accused Drona.

'That is a grave accusation indeed! Today, I shall kill at least one of the brave warriors amongst the Pandavas,' Drona promised, having been cut to the quick by Duryodhana's insult.

Drona constructed a wheel-shaped battle-order. Only Arjuna could get into this and come out. Susharma, the king of Trigarta, kept Arjuna busy on the other end of the battlefield. Arjuna's son Abhimanyu had learned to enter this formation from his father but did not know how to come out. Further, Abhimanyu was only a boy. How could he be sent into this battle order? But the honour of the Pandavas would be shattered if they were unable to penetrate this formation.

Yudhishthira said, 'Abhimanyu, you go ahead and enter the formation and we will follow you. Don't worry.'

This was an opportunity for Jayadratha who had been insulted during the kidnapping of Draupadi. This was his chance to take revenge by Shiva's boon, one day he would be able to defeat all the Pandavas except Arjuna.

Once Abhimanyu entered, Jayadratha stood at the mouth of the wheel-like formation and warded off all the other Pandavas. Abhimanyu displayed unequalled valour and fought against the brave Kaurava warriors all by himself.

'He is indeed his father's son,' Drona applauded him silently.

Karna was outwitted by Abhimanyu's attacks. Dushasana and Shalya lost consciousness. Drona, Kripa, Ashwathama, Vrihaddal, Kritavarma were unsettled by Abhimanyu's prowess. When Duryodhana's son Lakshman was killed by a lance thrown by Abhimanyu, Duryodhana, angered, ordered, 'Kill him by any means.'

Then all the warriors and great warriors sacrificed their good judgment and attacked Abhimanyu. They broke the rules of the war. The boy fought alone, all day and died.

Killing Jayadratha

The Pandavas were distressed at the death of Abhimanyu. Arjuna had been out; when he returned to the camp and heard the news, he lost consciousness. When he regained consciousness, he was like a fireball. The light of revenge shone in his eyes! His face hardened as he vowed, 'I will kill the sinner Jayadratha by sunset tomorrow or I will sacrifice myself in the fire.'

The news of his vow reached the Kaurava camp. Drona formed a complicated battle order of three concentric circles to hide Jayadratha from Arjuna.

Jayadratha's father had earned the boon that whoever would drop his son's head on the ground would have his own head severed from his body. Krishna knew of this boon and informed Arjuna.

But where was Jayadratha? The day was coming to an end. The Kauravas assumed that Arjuna would have to sacrifice himself. But Krishna used his illusory powers to cover the sun. Everyone thought that the sun had set. The Kauravas danced in joy.

Jayadratha came in front of Arjuna and began bragging. By Krishna's directions, Arjuna cut off his head and dropped it into the lap of his father.

Vriddhakshetra, Jayadratha's father was deep in meditation. Startled, he dropped the head to the ground and was beheaded himself.

Krishna removed the illusory clouds. The sun rays were visible again. Everyone understood—this was all Krishna's doing.

Killing Ghatotkach

When Jayadratha, the husband of his only sister, Dushala, was killed,

Duryodhana questioned Drona's loyalty. Drona said, 'You are unnecessarily suspicious of me, Duryodhana. Why don't you understand that I have grown old? My eyesight is not that clear, my hands tremble. Even then, I am trying my hardest. Well, why don't you declare that the fighting will continue all night?'

Ghatotkach, the son of Bheema and Hirimba was the hero of that war. He harassed all the Kauravas including Karna. It is said that anger makes you lose your judgment. Karna, incensed, lost his judgment and threw the Shakti arrow (which never fails to hit its target) and killed Ghatotkach. Indra had given Karna the Shakti arrow in exchange for his armour and earrings. Karna had saved this arrow, with great care, to kill Arjuna.

With the fall of Ghatotkach, everyone in the Pandava camp was down in the dumps. But Krishna looked happy because he knew that Karna would not be able to kill Arjuna.

Ashwathama—the elephant—is killed

The next day Dhrupad, Virata and other brave warriors lost their lives to Drona. Krishna said, 'We have to send the news of Ashwathama's death to Drona by some cunning means. He will not drop his arms until he hears of his son's death; as long as Drona continues to fight the Pandavas have no hope of victory.'

The king of Malav had an elephant called Ashwathama. Bheema attacked him with a club and killed him. Then he went and told Drona, 'Ashwathama is dead.'

Drona said, 'I do not believe anyone except Yudhishthira.'

Yudhishthira would not lie. Krishna explained to him in various ways, 'O king! Kshatriyas can use craft and power and artifice if necessary. There is nothing wrong in that.'

Yudhishthira went up to Drona and said very loudly, 'Ashwathama is killed.' Then under his breath he said, 'the elephant.' Thus Yudhishthira was kept from telling a lie and Drona was made to believe that Ashwathama was killed; the objective was fulfilled without much difficulty.

Drona gave up his arms. Dhristadyumna used a scimitar to behead Drona.

Absolutely infuriated, Ashwathama threw the weapon Narayani. This weapon would kill anyone who was riding a chariot, elephant or horse; it would also kill anyone carrying a weapon.

Krishna knew this; so by his instructions the Pandavas and their soldiers jumped down on the ground and cast off their weapons.

Duryodhana said, 'Ashwathama, throw the Narayani arrow again.'

Ashwathama said, 'No, the way this weapon works is that if this arrow is thrown a second time it will kill the person throwing it. The Pandavas were saved by Krishna today.'

Karna Parva

The vows of Karna and Arjuna

On the sixteenth day Duryodhana nominated Karna as the general of his troops.

The next day, Karna said, 'Today either Arjuna will survive or I will.'

Hearing this, Duryodhana was overjoyed. He asked Shalya to be Karna's charioteer. Shalya had once promised Yudhishthira that in the battle between Karna and Arjuna he would help Arjuna. This was Shalya's opportunity. So he agreed.

Although Karna displayed great valour on the battlefield and showed great pride, Shalya put him down and ridiculed him. Shalya's aim was to distract Karna.

When hit by Yudhishthira's arrow, Karna lost consciousness. But when he recovered Karna and the others taught Yudhishthira such a lesson that Yudhishthira gave up battle and retired to his camp.

When he heard the news, Arjuna and Krishna came running to see Yudhishthira. Yudhishthira said, 'Arjuna! Do not make such lofty claims regarding killing Karna. You had better give away your bow and arrow.'

'What! How can you insult me like that?' Arjuna rushed towards Yudhishthira with his scimitar.

Krishna caught hold of Arjuna's hand and deterred him. 'Arjuna, shame on you. What are you doing? Have you gone mad?'

Arjuna said, 'I have to kill anyone who will ask me to give away my bow and arrow. This is my vow. I am a Kshatriya. I have to honour my vows! So let me abide by my principles, Krishna.'

Krishna said, 'Do not speak to me of principles. Drop your scimitar. I hope I won't have to learn about principles from you. Whatever holds a person up are his principles. Whatever propels him towards greed, anger, lust, wine, ignorance is against all morality.

Arjuna was ashamed and repentant. He begged forgiveness from Yudhishthira. He said, 'Today either Karna's mother or Arjuna's mother will lose her son.'

Alas Arjuna! You are unaware that you both have the same mother, Kunti; Karna is your oldest brother.

Bheema kills Dushasana

Dushasana killed Bheema's charioteer, breaking the rules of battle. Infuriated, Bheema jumped into battle against the Kauravas. Dushasana was hurtled away by the blow of the club. Bheema sat on his chest and said, 'Do you remember trying to pull Draupadi's hair and disrobing her? Do you remember mocking me by calling me a cow? Today you will be punished for that. I will tear your flesh and drink your blood. If anyone dares they can try and stop me.'

When the Kauravas saw Bheema drinking blood they ran away in fear. Bheema said, 'I will kill that other sinner, Duryodhana, and then I shall be in peace.' That day another ten brothers of Duryodhana were killed by Bheema.

Killing Karna

As soon as Arjuna saw the young Vrishasena, he was reminded of Abhimanyu. To take his revenge he killed him with one arrow.

Karna, outraged, attacked Arjuna fiercely. The earth began to tremble as Arjuna and Karna were locked in battle. Everyone ran helter-skelter in fear.

Ashwasena, the son of Takshak, had wanted to take revenge for the incident at Khandava. Karna packed him into an arrow and hurled it at Arjuna.

Krishna applied some pressure with his foot and made Arjuna's chariot sink into the ground. A part of Arjuna's crown was singed but he was unharmed.

Using one arrow after another, Arjuna harassed Karna. Karna's crown and armour were shattered. Karna knew of many miraculous weapons but today he could not remember a single one. Also, the wheels of his chariot began sinking into the ground.

Karna remembered Parasurama's curse. Karna had become Parasurama's disciple by pretending to be a Brahmin. One day, Parasurama was sleeping with his head on Karna's thigh. A leech pierced Karna's thigh from one end to another but thinking that his teacher's sleep would be disturbed, Karna tolerated the pain in silence.

When Parasurama awoke he saw that the room was full of blood stains. Parasurama was perturbed, 'Karna, what has happened to you? Why did you not call me?'

Karna, oppressed by Parasurama's volley of questions told him the whole story. Parasurama said, 'You must be a Kshatriya. A Brahmin cannot have the power to bear so much pain.' Karna accepted.

Parasurama cursed Karna. 'For deceiving your preceptor, you will forget all the divine weapons when necessary.'

Karna also remembered the curse of the Brahmin. He had killed a calf belonging to the Brahmin. The Brahmin had cursed him, 'At a time of emergency the wheels of your chariot will sink to the ground.'

Now, both curses were coming true.

'Arjuna let me fix the wheel of my chariot. Do not throw an arrow at me now. This is not the principle of the Kshatriyas.' Karna appealed earnestly.

'Now you are uttering many lofty sentiments about moral principles. Where was your moral sense all these days?' Krishna asked.

Even after much pulling and tugging, the wheel of the chariot could not be fixed. It began to sink more and more. Thus Karna had to fight from the ground but he could not carry on for long. Arjuna's Anjalik arrow decapitated the brave but conceited Karna.

Shalya Parva

Duryodhana escapes to Dwaipayan

Shalya became the general on the eighteenth day of battle. Yudhishthira fought with great valour and killed Shalya. Only a few Kuru soldiers were left.

When he saw that there was no way out, the tired and injured Duryodhana escaped to Lake Dwaipayan. When Kripacharya, Ashwathama and Kritavarma heard the news they went to meet Duryodhana. Ashwathama said, 'O king, please come with us! Either you will die in the battle and go to heaven or you will win the war and enjoy the kingdom.'

Duryodhana said, 'I am very tired today. Let me rest tonight. Tomorrow I shall join the war.'

Three hunters who brought meat for Bheema heard this. They rushed to Bheema to give him the news.

Bheema breaks Duryodhana's thigh

The Pandavas, along with Krishna, rushed to Dwaipayan. Duryodhana had made an illusory water-spout and was hiding inside it.

'Suyodhana!' Yudhishthira always called Duryodhana by this name. He said, 'Come out Suyodhana. After having had everyone in the family killed, for you to hide away now does not look good. Come and fight like the brave.'

'Brother, I do not want the kingdom, I will become a hermit and go away to the forest,' Duryodhana pleaded.

'How can that be?' Yudhishthira said. 'We had only wanted five villages for the five brothers. Then you had said, "Without war I shall not give away even the piece of land that sticks to the end of a needle." Suddenly, overnight, how have you developed such stoicism?'

Duryodhana was pierced by Yudhishthira's criticism. He got ready with his club. Bheema was also ready.

Balarama came rushing. He said, 'If you must fight, fight in Kurukshetra, why here?'

There, after a fierce fight, Bheema hit Duryodhana on his left thigh and upheld his promise. Duryodhana's left thigh was broken. Then Bheema put his foot on Duryodhana's head and said, 'This is your punishment for asking Draupadi to sit on your thigh and calling me a cow.'

Balarama chased Bheema with a plough. In a war of clubs, it is against the rules to attack below the waist. Krishna explained to Balarama, 'What will Bheema do? He had to keep his promise. It is the duty of a Kshatriya to honour his promise.'

Sauptika Parva

Killing in the dark in the Pandava camp

Kripacharya, Ashwathama and Kritavarma saw Duryodhana lying with a broken thigh and began to cry. At Ashwathama's request, Duryodhana made him the general. The three of them, the general Ashwathama, Kripacharya and Kritavarma took refuge in a forest. Kritavarma and Kripacharya slept at night but sleep eluded Ashwathama. Suddenly, Ashwathama saw that an owl appeared, quietly moved from branch to branch, killed the baby crows and flew away very quietly.

Ashwathama's eyes lit up with the fire of revenge. He awoke Kripacharya and Kritavarma and said, 'Like the preying owl, we have to kill the Pandavas in the darkness of the night.'

The old Kripacharya did not agree. But Ashwathama wanted to kill his father's killers by hook or by crook. Finally his will prevailed.

Mahadeva was guarding the entrance to the Pandava camp. Inside, everyone was in deep slumber. Ashwathama began to pray to Shiva. Shiva was pleased; he said, 'Ashwathama, what can I say? Their time has come. Here, take the sharpened scimitar. You are just a pretext.'

Ashwathama first killed his father's killer Dhristadyumna. Then he killed whoever he found in the dark. Mistaking Prativindhya and the five sons of Draupadi for the Pandavas, he killed them.

Duryodhana dies

The cruel Ashwathama rushed to Duryodhana and told him the news. Duryodhana, at this point, was being eaten by foxes and the tigers. He heard this news and expressed much gratitude to Ashwathama before he died.

I want Ashwathama's jewel

Draupadi was beside herself with anger and sorrow. 'I want the jewel from Ashwathama's head,' she said. Ashwathama had a jewel on his head that shone brightly.

Ashwathama was found amongst Vyasdeva and the other sages, on the banks of the river Ganga. Chased by Bheema, Ashwathama threw the heavy-duty Brahmasira missile. Arjuna, in return, threw the same missile. The attack and counter-attack of the two Brahmasira missiles almost caused a cataclysm. Vyasdeva and Narad came rushing. They said, 'Take back your missiles; otherwise there will be widespread destruction.'

But the Brahmasira, once thrown, could not be taken back. So it was decided that Arjuna's Brahmasira would pull out the jewel from Ashwathama's head and Ashwathama's Brahmasira would kill Abhimanyu's child growing in Uttara's womb. But Krishna was to return him to life. This child was Parikshit. Things worked according to plan. Bheema gave the jewel to Draupadi. The immortal Ashwathama, having lost his jewel, retreated to the forest.

Stri Parva

Sorrow and the last rituals

Sanjay, Vidura, Vyasdeva, Kripacharya and Kritavarma consoled Dhritarashtra who was mourning the loss of his son. Everybody was in tears and as they prayed for the peace of the departed soul they walked towards Kurukshetra.

Yudhishthira came to meet Dhritarashtra with Krishna, Draupadi and his four brothers. After having blessed him, Dhritarashtra said, 'Where is Bheema? Do send for him.'

Krishna had anticipated this turn of events. He pushed forward an iron statue of Bheema. Dhritarashtra embraced the statue with such force that it smashed into pieces. 'What have I done?' Dhritarashtra broke down in repentance. Krishna assured him and said that Bheema was alive. Dhritarashtra was ashamed but relieved.

Gandhari said, 'Were all my sons so bad—could you not have let one of them live?'

Yudhishthira said, 'Mother, curse me, I am that heartless person who is responsible for the death of your one hundred sons. I do not want to continue with this life.'

Gandhari embraced Yudhishthira and blessed him. Then, opening the covering of her eyes, she saw the faces of her sons for the first and the last time.

While praying for the departed souls in the river, Kunti told the Pandavas about the true identity of Karna. In their sorrow they reacted to Kunti in anger, 'Why did you not tell us this earlier? Why are you such a cruel mother? We would have cherished our brother—the bravest of the brave.' Kunti dissolved into tears.

Shanti Parva

Yudhishthira was crowned king. Keeping Dhritarashtra at the head of things, responsibilities were delegated to various people and the Pandavas left to see Bhishma.

Anushasana Parva

Bhishma goes to heaven

Bhishma was lying on the bed of arrows, waiting for death. The Pandavas touched his feet, sat by him and took valuable advice from him about kingship, truth, sin and duty over the course of a few days.

Yudhishthira asked, 'Grandfather, what is moral principle?'

Bhishma said, 'If you do not want something to be done to you, do not do that to anyone. In brief, that is the moral principle for human beings.'

Arjuna, seeing tears in Bhishma's eyes, asked Krishna, 'Krishna, grandfather is so knowledgeable yet he has tears in his eyes. Is he crying out of sorrow?'

Krishna said, 'Why don't you ask him?'

Bhishma said, 'Krishna, you know what is making me cry. You are the greatest refuge for the Pandavas, yet even their sorrows know no bounds. I could not understand the true meaning of your actions and that is why I am crying.'

After spending fifty-eight days on the bed of arrows, Bhishma accepted his own death, according to the boon granted by his father in the month of Magha on the fortnight of the waxing moon.

All the arrows, miraculously, detached themselves from his body. The gods showered flowers from the sky. The eighth Vasu returned to heaven after having lived out his curse.

Ashwamedhika Parva

According to the advice of Vyasdeva, Yudhishthira organized an Ashwamedha Yagna.

Arjuna started to travel with a powerful horse. The kings of most of the kingdoms accepted Yudhishthira's suzerainty by putting up a brief fight or not fighting at all. In Manipur, Arjuna was almost killed by the arrow of Vabrubahana, Arjuna's son by Chitrangada. Ulupi, another wife of Arjuna, rejuvenated him by feeding him the nectar of life.

The horse of the yagna travelled to all the countries and returned victorious. The Ashwamedha Yagna was completed with great pomp and grandeur.

Ashramavasika Parva

Dhritarashtra goes to the forest

Sometimes Bheema would speak ill of the Kauravas. This would hurt Dhritarashtra. One day he informed Yudhishthira that he wanted to go to the forest with Gandhari to meditate there. Kunti said, 'The old king cannot see; Gandhari is blindfolded. I will go with them and help them find their way.' Vidura also accompanied them.

One day Vidura sat down to meditate and abandoned his earthly body. It was then that everybody found out that Dharma had been reborn as Vidura. One day, Dhritarashtra, Gandhari and Kunti sacrificed themselves in the forest fire while meditating.

Mausala Parva

The destruction of the Yadu dynasty

Thirty-six years of Yudhishthira's reign elapsed. The Yadavas became depraved and degenerate.

One day, they dressed a boy up as a girl, brought her to the saints and asked, 'Will she have a boy or a girl?' Furious at their impudence, Vishwamitra, Kanva and Narad cursed them, saying that this person would give birth to a mallet which would be the cause of their destruction.

One day, something that began as a verbal disagreement amongst the Yadavas about the battle of Kurukshetra led to a brawl: the boy actually gave birth to a mallet. From the mallet tall reeds grew. The inebriated Yadavas began to attack one another with the reeds and they were all killed; the boy who gave birth to the mallet was Krishna's son Shamba.

Krishna gave Arjuna the responsibility of looking after the old people and the women of the Yadu dynasty and went to look for Balarama. At one place he saw that Balarama had passed away after issuing a hundred-headed snake from his mouth.

Krishna lay down, weary, and was contemplating on the Yadu dynasty. A hunter Jara, mistaking him for a deer, shot an arrow at him. The arrow pierced his heel. Krishna's span on earth ended; the protagonist of the *Mahabharata* departed.

While protecting the Yadava women, Arjuna found out that he had grown old. Bands of robbers were abducting the women and he was unable to stop them. He was weak and his hands were trembling. Vyasdeva suggested, 'Arjuna, the time has come for all of you. You should proceed.'

Mahaprasthanika Parva

The great journey of the Pandavas

Having crowned Abhimanyu's son Parikshit king, Yudhishthira, his brothers and Draupadi began their great journey. A dog appeared and joined them. By the orders of Lord Agni, Arjuna returned his special bow and arrow to Varuna.

While negotiating the difficult terrain of the Himalayas, Draupadi fell.

Bheema said, 'O king! Draupadi was full of moral virtue. She was a good and a chaste wife. Why did she fall?'

Yudhishthira said, 'Draupadi was always partial to Arjuna. In her heart she loved Arjuna more than her other husbands. That is why she has fallen.'

Sahadeva fell a little while later. When Bheema wanted to know the reason for Sahadeva's fall, Yudhishthira said, 'Sahadeva thought that he was the cleverest. That is why he has fallen.'

Next Nakula fell. Yudhishthira said, 'Nakula thought he was the most handsome. Pride led to his fall.'

Next it was Arjuna's turn. Yudhishthira said, 'Arjuna would say that he would alone exterminate all the enemies but was unable to keep his word. That is why he has fallen.'

Then Bheema himself dropped down. Yudhishthira said, 'You ate too much. You boasted about your own strength without truly knowing the strength of another. That is why you have fallen.'

Only Yudhishthira and the dog were left. Suddenly Indra came down in his chariot from heaven. He said, 'Come aboard. You are going to heaven.'

Yudhishthira said, 'I do not want to go to heaven alone, leaving behind my four brothers and Draupadi.'

Indra said, 'They have all left their earthly bodies and ascended to heaven. You will go to heaven with your physical form intact. You will meet them all in heaven.'

Yudhishthira said, 'I will take this dog with me.'

Indra said, 'You are going to heaven on the strength of all your acts of piety. But how will the dog go to heaven?

Yudhishthira said, 'I have given shelter to this dog and he has been my trusted companion along the long journey. I can give up heaven but I cannot give up this dog.'

The dog then took the form of Dharma and appeared in front of Yudhishthira. He said, 'Yudhishthira, praise be to your virtue. I was only testing you. Come to heaven.'

Svargarohana Parva

Yudhishthira was most surprised when he reached heaven. He saw that the sinner Duryodhana has already reached there.

'How is this possible? There are no evil acts that Duryodhana has not committed. He cheated in dice and banished us to the forest. He insulted Draupadi and poisoned Bheema. He killed Abhimanyu while he was helpless. What has he not done? And he has the honour of being in heaven?' Yudhishthira asked Narad.

Narad said, 'O king! In heaven you must forget all such divisions. There is only friendship here; no one is your enemy.'

Yudhishthira was sarcastic. 'Well then, to which abode have my brothers, who are honest and good, and my virtuous wife been sent? It must be a higher abode.'

Yudhishthira was taken where his close relatives belonged. The road was dark and full of noxious smells. It was slippery with blood and corpses. Yudhishthira said, 'How much farther?'

Indra's messenger said, 'O great king! I have been instructed to take you only as far as you want to go.'

Yudhishthira said, 'Come messenger, let us return. I will not stay here another moment.'

'No, o great king! Please! Do not return! Stay a while longer! Your presence fills us with peace.'

'Who? Who speaks?'

'O great king! I am Bheema.'

'I am Arjuna.'

'I am Nakula.'

'I am Sahadeva!'

'I am Draupadi!'

'I am Karna!'

'What is this? Is it really all of you? Messenger, go to Indra and find out what sins they have committed that they have to stay here?'

Indra came. Dharma came. The whole place became fragrant. Indra said, 'O great king! They have been placed in hell according to the sum total of their actions. You have been placed in heaven. Please let us proceed there.'

Yudhishthira said, 'I do not want a heaven where there is no place for my brothers, Draupadi and my dear relatives.'

Suddenly the nightmarish surroundings disappeared. There was beauty and grace everywhere. Dharma said, 'O great king Yudhishthira, I was testing you again. I wanted to understand the depth of your love for your brothers and your own people. There is nothing to be afraid of; all your relatives are in heaven. I told you that when you climbed on to the heavenly chariot.'

'Then what was I witnessing all this while?'

'What you saw was the illusion of hell which Indra had constructed to test you. I have tested you thrice. You have passed with flying colours each time.'

'How is that?'

I tested you in the guise of a crane the first time and the second time in the guise of a dog. And this was the third test—you were tested by being shown a false hell.

'Why did I have to see the false hell at all?'

'When Drona was killed, you said, "Ashwathama is dead!" loudly but you said "an elephant" softly, under your breath, so that Drona could not hear you. So you had to see this illusion of hell once.'

'Was Duryodhana also made to see hell?'

'No!'

'Why?'

'That is because those who commit many sins and only a few charitable acts are first made to experience some heavenly pleasures and are then condemned to endless hell. Those who are mostly virtuous but commit a few sins are first made to experience hell and then allowed to live in heavenly surroundings.'

'What pious acts can Duryodhana be associated with?'

'Although Duryodhana is evil, he is fearless. Fearlessness is a virtue amongst Kshatriyas.'

'Come, o great king, let us go to the abode of Vishnu.'

'Come!'

When he came to Vishnu's abode Yudhishthira saw that Krishna was sitting and chatting with his four brothers and his wife. When they saw Yudhishthira they stood up as a mark of respect. Krishna and the others came and touched his feet. Yudhishthira was relieved to know the whereabouts of Bhishma, Drona, Kunti, Madri, Pandu, Dhritarashtra and the others. He was delighted to find out that Draupadi was the incarnation of the goddess Lakshmi.

Everyone lived happily ever after in heaven. The story of the _Mahabharata_ ends here.

The *Mahabharata* in Brief

For those who have very little time in hand and for those who cannot spend more than five or ten minutes to find out what transpires in the eighteen episodes of the *Mahabharata*, an outline of each of the episodes is presented here.

Adi Parva

The birth of the Kauravas and the Pandavas. Their fights during play. The ball falling into the well. Dronacharya is appointed the teacher of the princes. Ekalavya's gift to his teacher. Dronacharya tests his students. The princes display their skills in an open field. Yudhishthira gets the kingdom. Duryodhana's conspiracy. The house of lac. The Pandavas escape through a tunnel. Killing the demons, Hirimb and Bak. Draupadi's swayamvar. Arjuna hits the target. The five brothers marry Draupadi. The Pandavas return to Hastinapur. The Pandavas travel to Khandavprastha or Indraprastha. A huge palace is constructed. Arjuna goes to the forest. Abducting Subhadra. Setting fire to Khandav.

Sabha Parva

The giant Moy builds a resplendent palace for the Pandavas. The Rajasuya Yagna. Killing Jarasandha. Duryodhana's envy and humiliation. The game of dice. Yudhishthira's defeat. Trying to disrobe Draupadi. Bheema's vow. Playing dice again. Yudhishthira is defeated again. The Pandavas set off to retire to the forest for twelve years and to live in disguise for the thirteenth year.

Aranyaka Parva

The conversation between Draupadi and Yudhishthira. Arjuna wins weapons from Mahadeva and Indra. Duryodhana is taught a lesson. Durvasa and his thousand disciples come as guests of the Pandavas.

Jayadratha abducts Draupadi. Karna gives his armour and earrings to Indra. The conversation between the crane and Yudhishthira.

Virata Parva

The five Pandavas and Draupadi are in King Virata's palace. Keechak is killed. Duryodhana tries to rob King Virata of his cows and is completely routed. The end of their life in disguise.

Udyoga Parva

The Pandavas send an envoy of peace to Dhritarashtra in hope of getting back their kingdom. The request is denied. Krishna tries to act as a messenger of peace but Duryodhana rejects it. Preparation for battle.

Bhishma Parva

The war begins. Arjuna is weak. Krishna's advice. Fierce battle headed by Bhishma. Bhishma is laid to rest on a bed of arrows with help from Shikhandi.

Drona Parva

Drona becomes general. Abhimanyu is killed. Jayadratha is killed. Ghatotkach is killed. Yudhishthira tells a lie. Drona is killed.

Karna Parva

Karna is the general. Shalya is the charioteer. Karna and Shalya do not see eye to eye. Bheema tears the flesh of Dushasana and drinks his blood. Karna is killed.

Shalya Parva

Shalya is the commander. Shalya is killed. Duryodhana hides in the lake Dwaipayan. Bheema fulfils his vow. He breaks Duryodhana's thigh. Balarama is angered.

Sauptika Parva

Ashwathama attacks the Pandava camp at night and kills indiscriminately. The Pandavas are steeped in sorrow. Duryodhana dies. Bheema steals the jewel on Ashwathama's head.

Stri Parva

Sorrow. The burning of the corpses. Dhritarashtra smashes the iron statue of Bheema to pieces. Gandhari curses Krishna.

Shanti Parva

Yudhishthira is crowned king.

Anushasana Parva

Bhishma's advice. Bhishma wishes for and brings about his death.

Ashwamedhika Parva

The Pandavas perform the Ashwamedha Yagna. Arjuna battles his son Vabrubahana.

Ashramavasika Parva

Dhritarashtra, Gandhari, Kunti, Sanjay and Vidura leave for the forest. Vidura passes away. Dhritarashtra, Gandhari and Kunti sacrifice themselves in the forest fire.

Mausala Parva

The Yadu dynasty comes to an end. Krishna and Balarama end their life on earth.

Mahaprasthanika Parva

Draupadi and the five Pandavas set out on their final journey. All except Yudhishthira fall and die.

Svargarohana Parva

Yudhishthira ascends to heaven in his full physical form and after a brief glimpse of hell is re-united with his relatives.

Some Interesting Facts About the *Mahabharata*

1. The *Mahabharata* is the world's longest epic. No other epic poem has so many verses or so many characters.

2. The composer of the *Mahabharata* is the great saint Krishna Dwaipayan Vedavyas, son of Parashar and Satyavati and father of Sukdeva. He composed the *Mahabharata* in Sanskrit, the language of the gods.

3. The *Mahabharata* has one hundred thousand verses.

4. The oldest epic is Valmiki's *Ramayana*; Vyasdeva's *Mahabharata* is placed right after that.

5. Scholars are not unanimous on the date of composition of the *Mahabharata*. According to scholars of the classics, the *Mahabharata* was written around 3000 BC; according to Prabodhkumar Sengupta, the battle of Kurukshetra can be dated back to 2449 BC. According to Bankim Chandra, however, the battle was fought around 1530 or 1430 BC; Balgangadhar Tilak, Jogesh Chandra Roy and others think that the Kurukshetra was fought around 1400 BC. European scholars are of the opinion that the war can be dated to 400 or 500 BC.

6. The hundred thousand verses of the *Mahabharata* are divided into eighteen episodes. They are:

   1) Adi Parva; The First Episode
   2) Sabha Parva; The Assembly Episode
   3) Aranyaka Parva; The Forest Episode
   4) Virata Parva; In the Land of Virata
   5) Udyoga Parva; Getting Ready
   6) Bhishma Parva; The Bhishma Episode
   7) Drona Parva; The Episode of Drona
   8) Karna Parva; The Episode of Karna
   9) Shalya Parva; The Episode of Shalya

10) Sauptika Parva; The Episode of the Night Battle
11) Stri Parva; The Episode of the Wives
12) Shanti Parva; The Episode of Peace
13) Anushasana Parva; The Episode of Instructions
14) Ashwamedhika Parva; The Ashwamedha Episode
15) Ashramavasika Parva; Living in the Ashram
16) Mausala Parva; The Episode of the Mallet
17) Mahaprasthanika Parva; The Final Journey
18) Svargarohana Parva; Ascent to Heaven

7. The reason for the fall of the Pandavas and Draupadi during the final journey:

Order in Which they Fell	Name of Person	Reason for Fall
1.	Draupadi	Favouring Arjuna
2.	Sahadeva	Proud of being the cleverest
3.	Nakul	Proud of being the most handsome
4.	Arjuna	'I will kill all my enemies in one day, there is no one as skilled in archery as I am.'—this was his pride.
5.	Bheema	Eating too much and bragging about his own strength without knowing about the strength of others

8. The names assumed by the Pandavas during their one year in disguise:

Real Name	Assumed Name	Role
Yudhishthira	Kanka	Playing dice with the king
Bheema	Vallabh	Cooking
Arjuna	Vrihannala	Teaching music and dance to Uttara
Nakul	Granthik	Looking after the stables
Sahadeva	Tantipala	Looking after the cows
Draupadi	Sairindhri	Maid-in-hand to Queen Sudeshna —she was her hair dresser, made garlands and dressed her up in fragrance.

9. Whose conch shell was which?

Krishna—Panchajanya
Yudhishthira—Anantvijay

Bheema—Poundrya
Arjuna—Devdatta
Nakul—Sughosh
Sahadev—Mani Pushpak

10. One 'akhouini' or division of the soldiers meant:

Foot soldiers 1,09,350
Horses   65,610
Elephants   21,870
Chariots   21,870
Total   2,18,700

11. Who was killed by whom in the battle of Kurukshetra (Indra's fall is worthy of mention):

Killer	Victim	Killer	Victim
Yudhi-shthira	Shalya	Dhristadyumna	Drona, Shalva
Bheema	Duryodhana and Gandhari's 100 sons	Ashwathama	Dhristadyumna, Draupadi's five sons, Parikshit (later brought to life)
Arjuna	Jayadrath, Karna, Vrishasena	Drona, Kripa, Karna, Ashwathama, Vrihaddal, Kritavarma, Dushasana's son	Abhimanyu
Saha-deva	Shakuni, Uluk	Another opinion —Drona, Kripa, Karna, Ashwath-ama, Shakuni, Jayadrath, Dushasana	Abhimanyu
Karna	Ghatotkach	Another opinion—Karna, Dushasana, Kripacharya, Duryodhana, Drona, Ashwathama, Jayadrath	Abhimanyu
Drona	Dhrupad, Virata		

12. The battle of Kurukshetra lasted for eighteen days.

13. After the war, only ten brave warriors, on both sides, were alive. They were Yudhishthira, Bheema, Arjuna, Nakula, Sahadeva, Satyaki and Krishna from the Pandavas' side and Ashwathama, Kripacharya and Kritavarma from amongst the Kauravas.

14. Hanuman participated in the battle of Kurukshetra. He sat on Arjuna's chariot and hollered so that the Kauravas were frightened out of their wits.

15. Vibhishana was present at Yudhishthira's Rajasuya Yagna. At first he did not want to touch Yudhishthira's feet. He said, 'I will not bow my head to anyone but Krishna because I have bowed my head to Lord Rama.' Then Krishna himself lay on the ground and touched Yudhishthira's feet. Then Vibhishana was ashamed and followed suit.

16. According to one school of thought, Ravana and Arjuna were locked in a battle in Kailash. Arjuna flogged Ravana and then let him go. The Pandavas were friendly with Ravana's stepbrother Kuber.

17. According to a preset condition, Arjuna had to go to the forest to lead a monastic life for twelve years when he interrupted intimate moments between Yudhishthira and Draupadi. But Arjuna hardly led a monastic life. He entered into one marriage after another and spent his time in his father-in-laws' houses.

18. Arjuna died at least twice before his fall in the final journey; once in the hands of Dharma disguised as a crane and again in the hands of his son Vabrubahana.

19. Although he had vowed not to touch any weapons, Krishna tried twice to attack Bhishma with his Sudarshan Chakra—once on the third day of the battle and once on the ninth day. According to the scholar Sukhamoy Bhattacharya Shastri, this incident occurred perhaps only once, on the ninth day. The third day may have been a retelling. Bhishma was, like Arjuna and Draupadi, a great devotee of Krishna. He wanted his favourite god to break his vow. He might have even vowed to make him do so. To honour the promise of his disciple who was also the ultimate devotee of truth, Krishna broke his pledge himself.

20. Aircrafts resembling modern-day aircrafts were in use during the time of the *Mahabharata*. King Shalva alighted from an aircraft, Souva, and fought against Krishna. Krishna used his Sudarshan Chakra to destroy the king and his aircraft. There is also a striking similarity between the aircrafts described in the *Ramayana* and modern-day aircrafts.

21. Ila, daughter of Vaivasat Manu, could be a man for one month and a woman for one month, according to a boon granted by Mahadeva.

22. Shikhandi was first born as a woman. Dhrupad, passing her off as a man, got her married to the daughter of King Hiranyavarma. Once the wife told her father of this, there was a battle between Dhrupad and Hiranyavarma. Shikhandi was about to kill herself when she decided to borrow masculinity from Sthunakarna, Kuber's spy. By Kuber's curse that loan was never repaid. Shikhandi remained a man and Sthunakarna became a woman.

23. Drona was perhaps the world's first test-tube baby; many babies were born outside the body in both the *Ramayana* and the *Mahabharata*.

24. Yudhishthira had heard the *Ramayana* from the saint Markandeya.

25. Unable to bear Draupadi's humiliation, Bheema had wanted to burn Yudhishthira's hand in the Kaurava court.

26. When Yudhishthira insulted Arjuna and his bow and arrow (Gandeeva), Arjuna had wanted to kill his brother.

27. After the Kurukshetra, two out of Dhritarashtra's 102 children were alive. They were Yuyutsu, his son by Saubali, and Dushala, his daughter by Gandhari.

28. At the time of Kurukshetra, Yudhishthira was sixty-five years old, Duryodhana and Bheema were sixty-four, Arjuna and Krishna were sixty-three, and Nakul and Sahadeva were sixty-two years old.

29. Life span:

Krishna—107 years (106+)
Yudhishthira—109 years (108+)
Bheema—108 years (107+)
Arjuna—107 years (106+)
Nakula—106 years (105+)
Sahadeva—106 years (105+)
Draupadi—100 years
Duryodhana—72 years (71+)
Abhimanyu—16 years

There are conflicting opinions on this, as on many other issues. We have accepted the statistics that seem the most reasonable.

30. At the palace of King Virata, other than their assumed names, the Pandavas had secret names to call one another by:

Name	Secret name
Yudhishthira	Jay
Bheema	Jayanta
Arjuna	Vijay

Nakul	Jayatsen
Sahadeva	Jayadval

It is worth pointing out that the word 'jay', meaning victory, has been included in all the names.

31. In order to avoid war, Yudhishthira had wanted the following five villages from Duryodhana: Kushasthala, Vrikasthal, Makandi, Varanavat and another village.

    According to another school of thought, the five villages were Panipat, Sonprastha, Indraprastha, Tilprastha and Bhagprastha.

32. Duryodhana's wife's name is not mentioned in the *Mahabharata*. In a play, 'Benisanhar', Duryodhana's wife was called Bhanumati. Bhanumati was very beautiful and her father was Chitrangad, the king of Kalinga. Duryodhana had forcibly abducted her from her swayamvar. It is doubtful that the depraved Duryodhana would have been satisfied with one wife.

33. In the Kurukshetra, the Bengali kings fought in favour of Duryodhana.

34. Before entering the kingdom of Virata, where the Pandavas lived in exile for a year, Yudhishthira prayed to the goddess Durga, just as Rama had done before he went into exile. Yudhishthira entered the kingdom of Virata with the blessings of the goddess Durga.

The Journal of Yudhishthira

Most of us are curious to know where the Pandavas spent the twelve years when they were banished from their kingdom and the course of events during that time.

If Yudhishthira had recorded his journal during that time and if the journal had survived, we would not have had to imagine the section; we would have had all the facts.

We have tried to draft in this section what might have been some of Yudhishthira's journal entries; I do not know whether the lump of clay intended to be something beautiful has only become a distortion.

Where We (the Pandavas) lived During our Banishment;
Our Life During the Twelve Years, in the words of Yudhishthira

Kamyak forest

Once we left Hastinapur, we travelled westwards. Walking through the forest, we reached Kamyak forest [currently near the Gulf of Kutch], the favourite haunt of saints and sages, on the banks of the river Saraswati. Krishna spent some time with us. Our days passed happily. Kamyak forest is indeed a beautiful place. We are thinking of spending the days of our banishment here.

Dwaita forest

After Krishna left for Dwarka, we came to the scenic Dwaita forest [in modern-day Deoband] in the village of Sahranpur. This forest is also on the banks of the Saraswati. Draupadi and I had a significant conversation one evening here and Vyasdeva gave me a lesson in Pratismriti here.

My four brothers and my wife, who are innocent, are paying a heavy price for my mistakes.

Kamyak forest again

We have returned to Kamyak forest. Venison is our staple diet here. Arjuna has gone to the abode of the gods to bring various weapons. My brothers, my wife and I are travelling to various shrines. Just as the saints had told us, we have earned great happiness by visiting the holy places.

Vadrika Ashram

At the end of the pilgrimage, Bheema, Nakula, Sahadeva, Draupadi and I came to the Vadrika ashram [this is located in modern-day Kashmir]. It is beautiful and peaceful.

Gandhamadan mountain

Four years have passed since our banishment. We have come to the Gandhamadan mountain [at the northern end of the Himalayas. According to classical opinions, the Gandhamadan was Mount Kailash.]. Arjuna has joined us again after acquiring more skills with weapons and music and dance in heaven. His father Indra has given Arjuna many divine weapons. We may need these later.

In the Himalayas

After this we travelled in the Himalayas. Here I answered many complex questions asked by Nahush and was able to satisfy him. Nahush had taken the form of a python as a result of a curse and seeing me has relieved him of his curse. Apparently this was, interestingly, pre-destined.

Kamyak forest again

We have returned to Kamyak forest. This is our third visit here. One day Krishna and Markandeya paid me a visit. We had an interesting, significant conversation.

Dwaita forest again

We have come, via Kamyak forest, to Dwaita forest again. This is our second visit here. Duryodhana had come here to witness our misery. He got into a fight with Chitrasena, the king of the gandharvas. By my orders, Bheema and Arjuna rescued Duryodhana, Dushasana and their wives. It was important to have done this. After all, they are our flesh and blood. During this stay we have spent a year and eight months here.

Last night I dreamt that the deer of Dwaita forest had come to plead with me not to kill all of them for our food. We will return to the Kamyak forest. It was a very peaceful place indeed.

Return to the Kamyak forest

We have come back to Kamyak forest from Dwaita forest. This is our fourth visit here. Vyasdeva came here and blessed us.

After a few days, we will have completed eleven years in banishment; after we have completed thirteen years in banishment we will get back all our wealth. One day, suddenly, Durvasa came as our guest with ten thousand disciples; this was Duryodhana's conspiracy of course. Krishna, responding to Draupadi's prayers, averted possible disaster.

One day Jayadratha tried to abduct Draupadi and was beaten up by Bheema. I let Jayadratha go; otherwise our cousin would have been widowed. That would have been unbearable for me.

Dwaita forest again

We have again returned to the Dwaita forest for the third time. Dharma, disguised as a crane, had taken the lives of Bheema, Arjuna, Nakula and Sahadeva. I satisfied the crane with replies to his various questions and the crane in turn returned my brothers to life.

We have completed twelve years in banishment; we will set off from here for Viratanagar. How the twelve years have flown! Now I realize that even our exile was necessary.

Some Interesting Places and Characters in the *Mahabharata*

I have compiled an alphabetical list of interesting and important characters, places and technical terms in the *Mahabharata*.

In this age of speed, the curious reader can, using this list, find out what he or she wants to about any character or place in the *Mahabharata*. For practical reasons we have not included every place and character in this compilation. If the reader is unhappy with this, the writer is even more so; I hope that such exclusions will be overlooked.

Abhimanyu

A brave warrior, he was ARJUNA's son by SUBHADRA. He was fearless and 'manyuman', meaning valorous, and so he came to be called Abhimanyu.

Barcha, the son of Chandra, the Moon, was born as Abhimanyu. Chandra had agreed to let go of his favourite son for only sixteen years. So Abhimanyu had to leave this world in a heart-rending manner, at the age of sixteen.

He was extremely courageous. If he had not died when he did he may have been the bravest of all the warriors in the *Mahabharata*. By UTTARA, the daughter of King VIRATA, Abhimanyu sired a son, PARIKSHIT. Parikshit carried on the Pandava lineage.

On the thirteenth day of the battle, Abhimanyu died fighting in the circular battle-formation masterminded by DRONA. He fought courageously against the seven warriors: KARNA, DUSHASANA, KRIPACHARYA, DURYODHANA, DRONA, ASHWATHAMA and JAYADRATHA. The seven warriors shamelessly broke all the rules of war and together attacked the young boy.

When the news of Abhimanyu's death reached the Pandava camp everyone including Arjuna broke down. Krishna knew that it was time for Abhimanyu to return to his father, Chandra. Arjuna vowed to kill Jayadratha as Jayadratha had blocked the mouth of the wheel and had not let any of the Pandavas enter the wheel to help Abhimanyu.

There is remarkable similarity between Abhimanyu and Taranisen, a character in Krittivasa's _Ramayana_.

Adhirath

A charioteer by profession, he was KARNA's adoptive parent and his title was 'suta'. He was DHRITARASHTRA's friend. Once, when his wife Radha went to bathe in the river Ganga, she saw a box float away. She pulled the box and when they opened it they found Karna in it. They brought him up with great love and care. During the archery display of the princes, Karna had touched Adhirath's feet and was ridiculed by BHEEMA. Bheema had called him, 'son of a suta'.

Adrishyanti

Grandmother of VYASDEVA and mother of PARASHAR. She was the wife of Shakti, the son of Vashishtha, the royal priest of Rama and his family.

Aired

Krishna's grandson, he was the son of Aniruddh and Kukudamati and husband of Usha, daughter of VAAN.

Akhouini

One akhouini meant an entire regiment. It included:

Foot soldiers	1,09,350
Horses	65,610
Elephants	21,870
Chariots	21,870
Total	2,18,700

Aksha (Game of dice)

This game is against the rules of the Shastra. King Nal and YUDHISHTHIRA lost everything by playing this game. The virtuous Yudhishthira lost twice to the crafty SHAKUNI. According to the _Brahma Purana_, Mahadeva was the creator of this game which he played, with dice, with Parvati.

Amba

Exquisitely beautiful, she was the eldest of the three daughters of the king of Kashi.

The king of Kashi had organized a swayamvar for his daughters. BHISHMA went there in search of a bride for his brother VICHITRAVIRYA.

Amba had, in her heart, accepted King SHALVA as her husband. Bhishma brought all the three daughters for Vichitravirya. But Amba later wanted to marry Bhishma as Shalva rejected her once she had been abducted by Bhishma. As Bhishma had vowed to remain single, he expressed his inability to marry. Amba went for advice to Bhishma's teacher Parasurama. Even on Parasurama's request Bhishma refused to break his vow. The teacher and pupil engaged in a battle, after which Parasurama took leave of Amba after admitting his inability to convince Bhishma. Amba cursed Bhishma that she would be the cause of his death in her next life. That was exactly as it happened.

Amba sacrificed herself in the fire. In the next life, she was born as Shikhandi and was the cause of Bhishma's death.

Ambalika

The youngest daughter of the king of Kashi and the mother of PANDU. Bhishma abducted her along with her sisters Amba and Ambika. Then he released Amba as she was betrothed to another and got Ambika and Ambalika married to Vichitravirya.

When Vichitravirya died without an heir, by the orders of her mother-in-law Satyavati, she was sexually united with VYASDEVA. At the moment of union, she saw his face and became pale; the child resulting from this union was thus pale. The boy was called Pandu.

Ambalika spent her old age as an ascetic.

Ambika

The second daughter of the king of Kashi. BHISHMA abducted her from their swayamvar, along with Amba and Ambalika, and married her to his brother Vichitravirya. Vichitravirya died young without giving birth to an heir. By the instruction of her mother-in-law, Satyavati, Ambika had intercourse with Satyavati's son before marriage, Vyasdeva. During intercourse, she kept her eyes closed to avoid seeing Vyasdeva's ugly countenance; the son born thus, DHRITARASHTRA, was blind.

Satyavati now instructed Ambika to be with Vyasdeva again. This time she did not go herself but sent her maid; Vidura was born of the union. Ambika spent the rest of her life as an ascetic, far removed from earthly cares.

Animandavya

He was punished by being made to sit on a stake as retribution for inserting, when he was a child, a blade of grass into the anus of a grasshopper. Once, a thief was running away after stealing when Mandavya, as he was called then, was in deep meditation. When the security guard asked him, 'Which way did the thief go?' he did not reply. So the guard took him to the king who punished him by putting him on a stake. After a while, the repentant king brought him down and begged forgiveness. But the edge of the stake could not be pulled out from his body. Since the ani (tip of the stake) was in his body he became Animandavya. He cursed Yama, 'Since you have given me a heavy punishment for a trivial wrong, you will be reborn on earth.' Thus Yama or Dharmaraj was born as Vidura.

Anjanparba

GHATOTKACH's son, killed by ASWATHAMA on the fourteenth day of the battle.

Anugita

During the Kurukshetra, Lord KRISHNA had narrated the Gita to Arjuna, but by the end of the war Arjuna had forgotten much of it. When Krishna was about to return to Dwarka, Arjuna wanted Krishna to narrate the Gita again.

Krishna said, 'That is not possible right now. I cannot repeat what I narrated as part of meditation at an auspicious moment. Instead, listen to what I told Kashaypa the Brahmin who earned divine grace.'

Krishna then set forth some ideas on faith, called the Anugita.

Anusuya

Anusuya had suckled Brahma, Vishnu and Maheswar and reared them with great affection. The three gods wanted to grant her a boon. Anusuya asked to be the mother of all three. Som was born as a part of Brahma, Vishnu was born as Dattatreya; Maheswar was born as DURVASA. When Rama came to the saint Atri's ashram in Chitrakoot, Anusuya gave Sita many presents including divine garlands, cosmetics, fragrances and ornaments.

Arjuna

The third Pandava, he was KUNTI's and PANDU's son, fathered by INDRA, the king of the gods. He was the greatest amongst the five PANDAVAS and KRISHNA's favourite friend and cousin. His actual name was Krishna as his complexion was dark. (krishna means dark). He was the son of Kunti whose other name was Pritha and therefore he was called Partha. He could use both hands equally skillfully to string the bow and shoot the arrow; therefore he was called Sabyasachi (meaning ambidextrous). Since he procured much wealth by conquering countries he was called DHANANJAY (one who wins much wealth). He never returned without winning a war, therefore he was called Vijay (meaning victory). He was born when the star Uttarfalguni was ascendant; therefore he was called Falgun. Indra gave him a sparkling crown; thus he was called Kiriti, meaning crown. He was extremely courageous and therefore he was called Jishnu (meaning victorious). The name Arjuna means one who is willing to do good work. He had conquered sleep and therefore he was called Jitendriya (one who has conquered his senses). He was DONACHARYA's favourite disciple. In order to bestow on Arjuna the honour of being the most proficient archer Drona wrongfully asked EKALAVYA to cut his thumb.

When asked to aim at an artificial bird on the branch of a tree, Arjuna was able to see only its eye. The others saw everything around the bird. Drona was pleased with Arjuna's concentration.

Drona had once gone to bathe in the river Ganga. A crocodile bit into his leg. He could have freed himself; but to test his disciples he shouted for help. When all his disciples were puzzled into inaction Arjuna used five arrows to cut the crocodile into bits. His teacher had not a scratch. Drona was very happy and gave Arjuna a divine weapon called Brahmasira. Everyone wanted to see how well the princes were trained in the use of weapons. There too Arjuna was the best; only KARNA could compete in the same class.

In order to avenge Drona's humiliation, the princes, under the leadership of Arjuna, imprisoned Dhrupad and brought him to Drona.

In the guise of a Brahmin, Arjuna had outdone many brave warriors to shoot the difficult target and win Draupadi at her swayamvar. In order to obey their mother's unwitting instruction all the five brothers garlanded Draupadi.

Once, a thief was escaping after having stolen a Brahmin's cow. Arjuna had to go into the armoury to bring weapons in order to catch the thief. YUDHISHTHIRA and DRAUPADI were then in an intimate embrace. According to a preset condition, when one brother was with Draupadi in a room, none of the other brothers could enter the room. The punishment for breaking this rule was steep—twelve years of monastic life in the forest; Arjuna had to undergo this. He lived in the forest but did not live a monastic existence.

One day while she was bathing in the Ganga, ULUPI, the daughter of serpents, pulled Arjuna away to the underworld. Ulupi, although married, wanted to marry Arjuna but Arjuna did not agree. They, however, spent a night together and IRAVAN was born.

Arjuna fell in love and married CHITRANGADA, the daughter of the king of Manipur; VABRUBAHANA was born. Arjuna spent three years in Manipur and then travelled on a pilgrimage. According to the *Ramayana*, during this period Ravana had once called Arjuna to battle. Arjuna beat him up mercilessly and then took pity on him and let him go; they even became friends. Arjuna then relieved five women of their curses and returned to Chitrangada. At Pravas, he abducted Subhadra according to Krishna's advice. He spent more than four years at the houses of his two wives.

Once, when Krishna and Arjuna were resting on the banks of the Yamuna after many water sports with their wives, Lord Agni appeared and asked for their help. He said, 'I have been hungry for a long time. Indra's friend Takshak lives in this forest. Every time I try to burn this forest Indra sends rain and the fire is extinguished. I need your help.'

Krishna and Arjuna were ready to help but they did not have any weapons. Agni asked Varuna for Gandeev, the famous bow and arrow, and gave it to Arjuna. He also gave two quivers with limitless arrows. He gave Krishna the Sudarshan Chakra and a club called KOUMODOKI.

Takshak was outside the forest. Agni set fire to the forest. Krishna and Arjuna rescued the giant artist MOY. At Krishna's request, the grateful Moy constructed a marvellous palace for Yudhishthira at Indraprastha. He gave Arjuna the conch shell named Devdatta.

Arjuna was unable to take revenge for Draupadi's humiliation right away. Like an injured snake he was seething in anger; he vowed to kill Karna.

At Yudhishthira's insistence, he went to his father Indra. Indra asked him to pray to Mahadeva. Mahadeva appeared in the form of a hunter. God and devotee were involved in a fierce battle over claims of a wild boar. Mahadeva was satisfied and gave Arjuna the Pashupat.

Arjuna learned dance and music from the gandharva Chitrasena. Urvashi came to express her love to him. Arjuna rejected her saying, said, 'Shame on you! You are like my mother.' URVASHI cursed him to lose his masculinity. Indra assured Arjuna, 'This curse is like a boon; it will facilitate your living in disguise.'

During their year of living in disguise, Arjuna took up the job of teaching music and dance to Princess UTTARA. He was called Vrihannala. His code-name, used exclusively amongst the brothers, was Vijay.

When Duryodhana and his cohorts came to steal cows from King VIRATA, Prince UTTAR went to battle with great flourish taking VRIHANNALA as his charioteer. During the battle, Uttar wanted to flee and Vrihannala revealed himself as Arjuna. Twelve years of banishment and another year of living in disguise had been completed; there was nothing more to be afraid of. Arjuna was recognized by his enemies by the arrows he shot.

During the Kurukshetra, Arjuna told Krishna, 'I do not want to gain my kingdom by killing my elders.' Krishna then narrated the Gita to Arjuna. Arjuna's inertness, his illusions were driven away. Arjuna himself fought like a hundred warriors. He was the source of fear amongst the Kauravas. ABHIMANYU's death struck a big blow for him. He vowed to kill JAYADRATHA. He could fulfill his promise through Krishna's sleight of hand. Otherwise he would have had to kill himself. Because he had a friend like Krishna he was able to make Bhishma lie on the bed of arrows and he was able to kill Jayadratha and Karna.

Arjuna was angered when Drona was sent to his death because of a half-truth. When Yudhishthira insulted his Gandeev, his bow and arrow, he was about to kill Yudhishthira.

Arjuna followed Yudhishthira's horse of the Ashwamedha Yagna. He was defeated by his son Vabrubahana's arrows. His son also lost consciousness. Hearing Chitrangada's wails, Ulupi brought the reviving nectar from the land of serpents, and helped resuscitate Arjuna.

When he was trying to rescue a widow of the Yadava dynasty from the hands of miscreants, Arjuna realized that he was not as strong as before. He had forgotten the application of the divine weapons. Now was the time to return.

He returned the Gandeev and the special quiver to the god Varuna.

When the time came for the great journey, the five Pandavas and Draupadi, accompanied by a dog, set off. After Draupadi, NAKULA and SAHADEVA, Arjuna fell.

Bheema asked Yudhishthira the reason for Arjuna's downfall. Yudhishthira said, 'Arjuna had promised that in one day, he would exterminate all his enemies but he was not able to live up to that promise. He was also boastful of the fact that there was no archer as skilled as he was. For these two reasons he has fallen.'

Arjuna was a character that fills the reader with wonderment. He was a great warrior and very knowledgeable as well. That is why Lord Krishna chose him as the audience for the Gita. Again, he was outstanding in the arts like music and dance. He was extremely devoted to his brother. He was the object of affection for Bhishma, Drona and Vidura. He demonstrated respect for a teacher.

Arjuna had three wives: Draupadi, Chitrangada and SUBHADRA. Ulupi and he had a son called Iravan but Ulupi was not his wife. Arjuna gave birth to three sons: Srutakarma by Draupadi, Vabrubahana by Chitrangada and Abhimanyu by Subhadra.

Abhimanyu's grandson JANMEJAY's grandson ASHWAMEDHDATTA is supposed to have been the last man to appear in the *Mahabharata*. Arjuna is believed to have lived for 107 years.

Ashwamedhdatta

The grandson of JANMEJAY, he is the last person in the *Mahabharata*; no one is referred to after him. His father was SATANEEK and his mother the daughter of the king of Videha.

Ashwasena

TAKSHAK's son. During the fire in KHANDAVA FOREST his mother tried to hide him in her mouth and escape; Arjuna beheaded his mother but Ashwasena was able to flee and save his own life.

During the battle between KARNA and ARJUNA in KURUKSHETRA, Ashwasena hid in the form of an arrow in Karna's quiver in order to take revenge for his mother's death. When Karna shot that arrow, the omniscient Krishna sunk Arjuna's chariot by pressing his foot. As a result, Arjuna was saved although his golden crown was singed.

Ashwasena returned to Karna and revealed his identity. Karna said, 'Thank you Ashwasena, but I cannot take your help. I do not use the same weapon twice and I do not want to be victorious with help from another.'

Disappointed, Ashwasena tried to battle his mother's killer by himself but was killed in the process.

Ashwathama

Son of DRONA and KRIPI, he was called Ashwathama because he had neighed like a horse (ashwa means horse) as soon as he was born. He is one of the ten immortal people. His father was his teacher in the use of weapons. Infuriated at the way his father was killed, Ashwathama shot the Narayanastra. Following KRISHNA's advice, all the Pandavas alighted from their chariots and dropped their weapons. This defused Ashwathama's weapon.

In the dead of night, in the absence of the PANDAVAS, Ashwathama went with KRITAVARMA and his maternal uncle KRIPA into the Pandava camp and killed the five sons of Draupadi along with DHRISTADYUMNA and SHIKHANDI. When BHEEMA heard the news, he chased Ashwathama. Ashwathama used the Brahmasira; so did Arjuna. Eventually, to bring about peace, Ashwathama's weapon killed Abhimanyu's son in Uttara's womb; the child was later resuscitated by Krishna. Ashwathama had to give up the jewel on his head. Bheema carried the jewel to Draupadi, as Ashwathama retired to the forest.

Aswini Kumaras

Physicians of heaven, they were the twin sons of Samjna, the daughter of Viswakarma and Surya. Samjna had taken the form of a mare during her union with Surya, so the twins were called Aswini kumara. Madri, using the mantra taught by KUNTI, invoked them to father her sons; the twins NAKULA and SAHADEVA were thus born.

Bajra

The grandson of Krishna's son PRADYUMNA. When the Yadu dynasty was destroyed, the PANDAVAS made him the king of INDRAPRASTHA.

Bajradatta

The son of King Bhagadatta of Pragjyotishpur. When he blocked the path of the horse of the Ashwamedha Yagna he was defeated by ARJUNA.

Bak

A fierce demon, he was the son of Alambush. BHEEMA killed him in EKCHAKRA.

Balandhara

Wife of Bheema and daughter of the king of Kashi. Her son was Sarbaga.

Balarama

He was an avatar of Lord Vishnu and the elder brother of KRISHNA. VASUDEVA's son, he was born of ROHINI.

Devaki's seventh son was sent by YOGMAYA to the womb of her sister and Vasudeva's wife Rohini's womb. He was forcefully kept in the womb so he was called Sankarshan (force). His weapon was the plough, so he was called Haladhar, Halayudh and Haliram (hal means plough).

He was also kept in Gokula with NANDA and YASHODA to save him from Kansa. Krishna and Balarama grew up together. He mastered all the Shastras. His teacher was the sage Sandipani. He killed Dhenukasara. He participated in the killing of Kansa.

When Bheema broke Duryodhana's thigh transgressing the rules of the fight, Balarama rushed to kill Bheema. Krishna stopped him. Bheema and Duryodhana learned to fight with the club from Balarama.

When Arjuna abducted SUBHADRA, he wanted to attack Arjuna but Krishna pacified him. When the Yadu dynasty was being destroyed, Balarama was sitting under a banyan tree and meditating. A white hundred-faced snake came out of Balarama's mouth and disappeared into the sea; Balarama's life on earth came to an end. A few days after this Krishna died, killed by a careless hunter.

Barcha

Chandra's favourite son. Chandra had let him go for sixteen years. He was born to the Pandavas as ABHIMANYU. After his untimely death in the battle he returned to Chandra.

Bhagadatta

The son of King Narakasura, the king of Pragjyotishpur. When he disobeyed YUDHISHTHIRA in the Rajasuya Yagna, ARJUNA defeated him and forced him to accept Yudhishthira's submission.

On the twelfth day of the KURUKSHETRA, to avenge his humiliation, he threw the Vaishnavastra, given by his father, at Arjuna. KRISHNA took the weapon on his chest. The weapon became a Vaijayanti garland and hung on Krishna's chest. Arjuna killed Bhagadatta.

Bhanumati

Wife of DURYODHANA. Duryodhana picked her up by force from her swayamvar and brought her to HASTINAPUR.

The incredibly beautiful Bhanumati had overlooked Duryodhana and many other kings by not garlanding them and they felt insulted. The arrogant Duryodhana could not swallow this ignominy. He abducted her and brought her to Hastinapur where they got married.

Bhanumati's father was CHITRANGAD, the king of Kalinga. He had invited many kings at the swayamvar. So it was not a very pleasant episode in Duryodhana's life; he had to fight with many kings.

Bhanumati was not named in the *Mahabharata*; she is mentioned in the play 'Benisamhar.'

Bhanumati and Duryodhana had two children, a son named Lakshman and a daughter named LAKSHMANA.

At the end of the Kurukshetra war, the Kaurava widows were steeped in sorrow. It can be assumed that Bhanumati's pain and sorrow was not less than that of the others.

Bharadwaj

DRONA's father and son of Vrihaspati. His other name was Vitath.

He was filled with lust when he saw Ghritachi having a bath. The semen from his ejaculation was stored in a pitcher. Drona, the first test-tube baby in the world, was born in that pitcher.

Vrihaspati forced himself on Mamata, the pregnant wife of Bharadwaj's elder brother Utathya. The child in Mamata's womb put out his leg and tried to stop his uncle. Vrihaspati's semen fell on the ground. The child born from that semen was abandoned by Mamata and Vrihaspati. Marudgan reared that child.

He was fed by Marudgan and therefore he was called Bhar (to be fed); he was born of two strengths and therefore he was dwaj or half-breed—Bhar and dwaj together form the word Bharadwaj. He is mentioned in both the *Mahabharata* and the *Ramayana*. Rama and Sita visited his hermitage on their way to the forest and on their way back.

Bheema (Bheemsena)

The second son of KUNTI and PANDU but born of Pavan; thus he was called Pavan Nandan. He was just a year younger than YUDHISHTHIRA and the same age as DURYODHANA. He had a fire in his belly; thus he could devour large amounts of food and was called Vrikodara (vrika means fire and udar means belly).

The KAURAVAs were always being outwitted by Bheema when they were young. To retaliate, they mixed poison in his rice pudding and fed it to him. They threw the unconscious body of Bheema into the Ganga. Vasuki, the king of serpents, fed Bheema, the grandson of his grandson KUNTIBHOJA, much 'amrit' and Bheema returned more powerful than before. The Kauravas were astonished and more envious. They kept looking for ways and means to teach the Pandavas a lesson. Bheema set fire to the house of wax where he and his brothers were meant to die. Bheema crossed difficult terrain with his mother on his shoulders, NAKULA and SAHADEVA in his lap and holding the hands of Arjuna and Yudhishthira.

He killed HIRIMB, who fed on human flesh, and married his sister, Hirimba. Bheema and Hirimba had a son Ghatotkach. Bheema also killed the rakshasha BAK at Ekchakra when he heard of his terrorizing the lives of the people there.

Bheema's patience reached his threshold when he watched Draupadi being humiliated. He asked Sahadeva to get a flame to burn the hand with which Yudhishthira played dice.

When Duryodhana, making a lewd gesture to DRAUPADI, patted his thighs, Bheema vowed that he would break his thighs in a club fight.

Dushasana pulled Draupadi by her hair and tried to disrobe her. Bheema promised that he would tear open Dushasana's chest and drink his blood. To save Draupadi from disgrace, it was Bheema who rushed to her rescue again and again.

Bheema vowed to kill all of DHRITARASHTRA's sons and, needless to say, he fulfilled his promise.

When he went to get a hundred-petalled lotus from the Gandhamadan mountain for Draupadi, he met his elder brother HANUMAN. Hanuman gave much valuable advice to Bheema. Hanuman helped the PANDAVAS in the KURUKSHETRA war by sitting on Arjuna's chariot which had a flag with the insignia of a monkey.

JAYADRATHA was caught by Bheema while trying to abduct Draupadi. Bheema beat Jayadratha to a pulp; if Yudhishthira had not forgiven him, Jayadratha would have been killed by Bheema that day.

At King VIRATA's palace, Bheema assumed the name of Vallabh and worked as a cook. His code name, used only amongst his brothers, was Jayanta. When the depraved Keechak, brother-in-law of Virata, insulted Draupadi, Bheema killed Keechak.

Bheema killed an elephant called ASHWATHAMA. It was the news of the killing of this elephant that Yudhishthira conveyed to Drona which facilitated the killing of Drona.

When Bheema filled his mouth with Dushasana's blood, everybody fled in fear from the battlefield, shouting, 'This is not a human being; he must be a rakshasha.'

Bheema knew well the rules of fighting with clubs. But to keep his promise he hit Duryodhana on the thigh and avenged Draupadi's dishonour.

GANDHARI's hundred sons were killed by Bheema; thus Bheema fulfilled his vows.

When Dhritarashtra wanted to embrace Bheema after the war, by Krishna's advice an iron statue of Bheema was put forth. Dhritarashtra, mistaking it for the real Bheema, smashed it to bits. Later, Dhritarashtra was reassured to hear that Bheema was alive.

Bheema and Arjuna were the main sources of strength for the Pandavas; their strength commanded everyone's respect.

After Yudhishthira became king, Bheema would subject Dhritarashtra and Gandhari to criticism; Yudhishthira would beg forgiveness every time, on behalf of Bheema. Eventually, the Pandavas left the palace and retired to meditate in the forest where they died.

During the final journey, as Draupadi, Sahadeva, Nakula and Arjuna fell, Bheema was surprised and asked Yudhishthira the reason for their falling. Finally, he also he fell and he asked Yudhishthira the reason for his falling.

Yudhishthira said, 'Excessive eating and bragging about your own strength without taking a true measure of the strength of others has caused your downfall.'

There is no doubt that Bheema was the bravest of the brave. It is not true, however, that Bheema did not know anything other than his elder brother and his club. The conversations amongst Yudhishthira, Draupadi and Bheema during their stay in the forest is proof of the depth of his knowledge.

Bheema had four wives: Hirimba, Draupadi, Balandhara and Kali. His son by Hirimba was GHATOTKACH; Draupadi's son with Bheema was Sutasoma; Balambara and Kali had given birth to Sarbaga and Sarvagata respectively.

Bheema lived for about one hundred and eight years.

Bhishma (Devavrata)

SHANTANU's son by GANGA, he was Dyu, one amongst the eight Vasus. One of the finest characters in the *Mahabharata*, he was second only to Krishna in importance.

A staunch devotee of Krishna, he led a monastic life and was truthful and virtuous. He learned the Vedas from Vashishtha and the art of using weapons from Parasurama.

The Vasu Dyu was born, by Vashishth's curse, to Ganga as Devavrata; he was cursed as he had stolen the sage's wish-cow NANDINI. After he was born Ganga took him back with her. She kept him with her for thirty-six years and taught him many things. Then she returned him to her husband Shantanu.

Four years later Shantanu was enchanted by the beauty of SATYAVATI, the daughter of Dasraj, and proposed to her. Dasraj had a condition—Satyavati's son would be crowned king. Shantanu then became anxious about being able to win Satyavati.

Devavrata learnt of the state of affairs from Dasraj. He said, 'I will never put forward my claim to the throne.'

'What about your children?' asked Dasraj.

'I will abstain from sexual pleasures; I will not marry,' Devavrata promised. Dasraj was convinced. The gods showered flowers from heaven. Shantanu blessed his son saying he would die only by his own will. Because of his terrible promise, he was called Bhishma. (bheeshan means terrible). He was committed to the truth so he was called Satyabrata (brata means firm resolve, satya means truth). He was called Gangeya because he was Ganga's son.

VICHITRAVIRYA and CHITRANGAD, Satyavati's sons, died when they were young. After Shantanu's death, Chitrangad became king and after his death Vichitravirya became the king. For his brother, Bhishma abducted from their swayamvar the three daughters of the king of Kashi, AMBA, AMBIKA and AMBALIKA, noted for their beauty.

Amba said that she had had a secret marriage with the king of Shalva. Bhishma let Amba go and gave the other two girls to his brother Vichitravirya.

The king of SHALVA did not accept Amba. Amba was also impressed by Bhishma's courage. She told him, 'You are responsible for my plight. You must marry me.' Bhishma told her about his inability to do so because of his vow. Amba was very persistent. She went to Bhishma's teacher, Parasurama. Satyabrata did not agree to break his promise even after his teacher instructed him to do so. There was a fierce fight between student and teacher. Narad and the others had to come to stop the fight. Parasurama told Amba, 'It is impossible to defeat Bhishma,' and left.

Amba cursed Bhishma, 'I will be the cause of your death in my next life.' She sacrificed herself to the fire. By Mahadeva's blessing, in her next life, she was born as Shikhandi, the emasculated son of Dhrupad.

The lustful Vichitravirya died of tuberculosis. Satyavati asked Bhishma to impregnate Ambika and Ambalika but because of his promise he refused. Vyasdeva, Satyavati's son out of wedlock, agreed to the proposition.

Dhritarashtra was born to Ambika, Pandu to Ambalika and Vidura to a maid of the palace. Bhishma brought them up and got them married. Since Dhritarashtra was born blind, Pandu became king. After Pandu's death, Dhritarashtra became king.

Bhishma first appointed Kripacharya and then Dronacharya to teach the princes the use of weapons. Bhishma loved all the princes very much but he was especially affectionate towards Arjuna. He also loved Yudhishthira for his adherence to the truth.

Bhishma had given good advice to Dhritarashtra to stop the war and the game of dice but to no avail.

He did not like Karna because he was arrogant and had incited Duryodhana to go against the Pandavas.

Bhishma had vowed to protect the throne of Hastinapur but he knew that the side which had Krishna in it would win. In his heart of hearts he supported the Pandavas.

His role during the game of dice and the disrobing of Draupadi is surprising and disappointing. For such a strong character to remain aloof upon witnessing such an incident is not seemly.

In the expedition to steal King VIRATA's cows, Arjuna beat Bhishma to a pulp. Duryodhana was completely defeated then.

Bhishma had promised Duryodhana that he would kill ten thousand Pandava soldiers everyday. But he would not kill the Pandavas or SHIKHANDI.

During the war, Bhishma was almost a hundred years old. But he fought so valiantly that the battlefield trembled.

Forgetting his promise, Krishna rushed towards Bhishma with his Sudarshan Chakra on the third and ninth day of battle. Arjuna stopped him. Bhishma, being a devotee of Krishna, was rather happy. He wanted to make Krishna break his vow; the god broke his vow to please the devotee.

It was impossible to kill Bhishma; it was also difficult to outwit him. By Krishna's advice, the Pandavas went to Bhishma to find out ways to defeat him. The next day, Arjuna went to battle and had Shikhandi sit in front of him. Seeing Shikhandi, Bhishma put down his arms. Arjuna hit arrow after arrow and made a bed of arrows for Bhishma.

When Bhishma wanted a pillow, DURYODHANA brought him a soft pillow. But it was not what Bhishma had wanted; Arjuna used an arrow to give support to Bhishma's head. When he was thirsty he did not drink the cold, fragrant water that the Kauravas brought for him. When Arjuna used the Varuna arrow to get cold water from the earth into Bhishma's mouth Bhishma was satiated. He blessed Arjuna with all his heart. He even forgave Karna. He gave good advice.

Bhishma lay in his bed of arrows for fifty-eight days. The valuable advice that he gave Yudhishthira for thirty days is called the 'Bhishma Gita'. The depth of his knowledge is evident from his advice.

In his final moments he said, 'Yato dharmastata jaya,' meaning victory comes to the virtuous.

This great hero of the _Mahabharata_ willed his death in the month of Magha on the eighth day of the waxing moon.

Bhishmak

The king of Bhoja and father-in-law of KRISHNA; he was the father of RUKMINI. His son was Rukmi. He was JARASANDHA's friend. SAHADEVA

fought against him and forced him to pay tax in Yudhishthira's
Rajasuya Yagna.

Bhuminjay

Another name for UTTAR.

Bhurisraba

Son of Somdatta, king of Kurur. Somdatta got him by Mahadeva's
blessings.

Bhurisraba killed the ten sons of Satyaki on the fifth day of the
battle of Kurukshetra. When Satyaki's grandfather Sini, a courageous
warrior of the Yadu dynasty, abducted DEVAKI, Somdatta, a valiant
warrior of the Kuru dynasty, was offended. Sini had kicked him; to
take revenge, Bhurisraba, son of Somdatta, kicked Sini's grandson
Satyaki. Bhurisraba rushed to behead Satyaki. Breaking the rules of
war, Arjuna used one arrow to cut off the right hand of Bhurisraba. To
protest, Bhurisraba sat in meditation to leave his earthly body. In this
state, ignoring everybody's advice, Satyaki beheaded Bhurisraba.

Chakravyuha

An impregnable battle order in the form of a wheel. Drona had
organized this formation on the day of the killing of ABHIMANYU.
Amongst the PANDAVAS, only ARJUNA knew how to pentrate this
formation and come out.

Abhimanyu only knew the way in; he did not know how to get out
and that is why he was helpless against the group of seven charioteers
and was killed by them.

Chitrangad

SHANTANU's son by Satyavati. He was the king after Shantanu died. He
died young at the hands of the gandharva Chitrangad.

Chitrangada

ARJUNA's wife and mother of VABRUBAHANA. She was the daughter of
the king of Manipur, Chitravahana. Arjuna left home to lead a
monastic life for twelve years but was stunned by her beauty and
married her. Arjuna's son by her was named VABRUBAHANA.

Chitrasena

He was a gandharva of heaven. He taught music and dance; ARJUNA
learnt these arts from him. He was the son of Viswabasu, the king of
the gandharvas.

Duryodhana and his courtiers had come to watch the PANDAVAS' misery in DWAITA FOREST and were imprisoned by Chitrasena. By YUDHISHTHIRA's instructions Arjuna fought against his guru Chitrasena and freed Duryodhana and the others.

Chedi

The land between the rivers Narmada and Godavari. SISUPALA was the king of Chedi, near the modern-day Jabalpore.

Chekitan

A valiant warrior of the Yadu dynasty.

Damghosh

King of CHEDI and father of SISUPALA, he was KUNTI's brother-in-law and KRISHNA's uncle.

Devavrata

Another name for BHISHMA.

Devika (1)

VIDURA's wife and daughter of Devaka. In those days, the child of a Brahmin father and a Sudra mother was called a Parsab. Since Vidura was a Parsab, Bhishma, according to the rules of the time, married him to a Parsab girl, Devika. Devika had many children whose names are not known.

Devika (2)

Also known as Devaki, she was the wife of YUDHISHTHIRA and daughter of Govasana, a worshipper of Shiva. In her swayamvar, she garlanded Yudhishthira. Yudhishthira's son by Devika was named YODHEYA.

Devyani

Daughter of Sukracharya and Uryashwati. Kach, the son of Vrihaspati, came to Sukracharya to learn the art of reviving the dead in order to defeat the asuras in the battle between the gods and the demons. Devyani fell in love with Kach but Kach did not want to marry her because students were not allowed to marry the daughter of their teacher. Devyani cursed him, 'When required you will not be able to use this learning on yourself.'

Kach cursed her back, 'No Brahmin will marry you.'

Devyani's friend SRMISHTHA had once thrown her into a well in a fit of anger. King YAYATI heard Devyani's cries and rescued her. As a punishment Sarmishtha had to become Devyani's maid.

When Devyani and Yayati got married, Sarmishtha also went to live with them. Devyani bore Yayati two sons—YADU and Turvasu. Yayati also had a relationship with Sarmishtha. Sarmishtha had three sons by Yayati: Druhya, Anu and Puru. Puru was the founder of the Puru dynasty and Yadu, the founder of the Yadu dynasty.

When Devyani came to know of the illicit relationship between her husband and Sarmistha, she informed her father. Sukracharya's curse caused Yayati to age prematurely. Sukracharya had also said that he could exchange his old age with someone's youth. No one agreed at first; finally Sarmistha's son Puru agreed. Yayati enjoyed his son's youth for a thousand years and then realized that there was no end to enjoyment. He returned his youth to his son and went to heaven.

Dhananjay

Another name for ARJUNA.

Dharmaputra

Another name for YUDHISHTHIRA.

Dhoumya

YUDHISHTHIRA's priest. Except for the one year when the PANDAVAS had to live in disguise, Dhoumya was always with the Pandavas, sharing in their joys and sorrows. He gave them valuable advice before that year of disguise.

Dhristadyumna

DHRUPAD's son who rose from the flames of the yagna, he was a disciple of DRONA. Going against the ethics of war, he killed Drona in the battle. At Draupadi's swayamvar, he explained the rules of shooting at the target. Satyaki, from his own camp, rushed to kill him because he killed Drona wrongfully. ASHWATHAMA killed him in the dead of night when he was sleeping in the PANDAVA camp.

Dhristaketu

Son of SISUPALA, he joined hands with the PANDAVAS in the KURUKSHETRA war. He showed exemplary courage on the day JAYADRATHA was killed. He was killed by DRONA.

Dhritarashtra

Born from AMBIKA's womb; son of VICHITRAVIRYA but born of another man, VYASDEVA. He was blind form birth. In his previous birth he was Hansanama, the head of the Gandharvas and son of Arista.

Ambika, seeing Vyasdeva's monstrous face, had closed her eyes during her union with him and this caused Dhritarashtra to be born blind. Because he was blind, he could not be the king even though he was older than his brother, who was crowned king. When Pandu died, DHRITARASHTRA became king.

In his blind love for his son, he committed sin after sin. He gave permission for all the heinous deeds of the Kauravas: sending the PANDAVAS to the house of wax, banishing them to the forest, inviting them for dice and then cheating. Good advice from BHISHMA, VIDURA, Krishna and Gandhari could not make holes in the solid wall of his affection for Duryodhana.

SANJAY, blessed with divine sight by Vyasdeva, gave a surprisingly objective commentary of the KURUKSHETRA war to Dhritarashtra. His heart bled for his hundred sons. At the end of the war he wanted to avenge his sons' death by killing Bheema but he managed to destroy only a statue of BHEEMA. After the Pandavas got the kingdom, Bheema's cutting comments pained Dhritarashtra. The old man retired to the forest with Gandhari. KUNTI, Vidura and Sanjay went with them. While he was meditating he was enveloped by the flames of a forest fire.

Dhritarashtra's conscience would prick him sometimes but he always buried it under his affection for his son.

Dhrupad

He was the king of Panchal, father of DRAUPADI and son of Pushat. He was also known as Rajyasen or Yagnasen. The five PANDAVAS were his sons-in-law.

Dhrupad was the childhood friend of DRONA. When he became king he insulted Drona. Drona had him imprisoned by the princes and avenged his humiliation.

In the Kurukshetra, Dhristadyumna, Dhrupad's son, beheaded Drona and took revenge for his father's dishonour. Again, Ashwathama killed the sleeping Dhristadyumna in the Pandava camp and took revenge for his father's death.

His children were SHIKHANDI, UTTAMOUJA, DHRISTADYUMNA and DRAUPADI.

Draupadi

She arose from the holy fire of the yagna performed by DHRUPAD, the king of PANCHAL. She was the wife of the five PANDAVAS. DHRISTADYUMNA, SHIKHANDI and UTTAMOUJA were her brothers, older to her. She was one of the five illustrious women.

She had a dark complexion and thus was also called Krishna (meaning black). She was Dhrupad's daughter and thus she was called Draupadi. She was the daughter of Yagnasen, another name for Dhrupad, thus she was Yagnaseni. She was the princess of Panchal; thus she was called Panchali.

The beautiful Draupadi garlanded ARJUNA at her swayamvar. But KUNTI's careless instructions made her accept the five brothers as her husbands.

When KARNA had come to shoot the target at her swayamvar, she had said that she would not marry the son of a charioteer. Karna never forgot that humiliation.

The brothers had made a rule that when one brother was spending time with DRAUPADI the other brothers would not enter the room. If they did enter they would have to live a monastic life in the forest for twelve years. As it happened, this punishment was meted out to Draupadi's favourite husband, Arjuna. When Draupadi was locked in an intimate embrace with YUDHISHTHIRA, Arjuna, to help a Brahmin, had to enter the armoury.

After losing everything in the game of dice, Yudhishthira also betted on Draupadi and lost. Duryodhana sent a messenger to Draupadi to bring her to court. The sharp Draupadi asked the messenger whether Yudhishthira wagered himself first or Draupadi? If he had wagered himself first and lost, then he did not have the right to wager Draupadi.

Draupadi had to face utter degradation at the royal court. Her brave husbands bowed their heads in shame. When Dushasana tried to disrobe her, she lost faith on her husbands and prayed to Krishna for help. Lord Krishna answered her earnest prayers and provided her with endless cloth. Dushasana, tired of pulling, sat down wearily. Vikarna, one of Duryodhana's brothers who had good sense, admonished Dushasana.

That day Draupadi raised many basic questions in court. The elders like BHISHMA and DRONA could not answer them; they simply listened with their heads bowed.

By Duryodhana's cunning, Durvasa and his ten thousand disciples once became the guest of the Pandavas when they were living in the forest. Durvasa was quick to curse. In answer to Draupadi's prayers, Krishna saved the Pandavas from inevitable disaster.

When Jayadratha tried to abduct Draupadi, Bheema wanted to kill him but Yudhishthira stopped him.

At the palace of King VIRATA, Draupadi took the responsibility of dressing Queen SUDESHNA's hair.

Draupadi also demonstrated her intelligence in the killing of KEECHAK.

ASHWATHAMA mercilessly killed Draupadi's five sons. Like all the other times, Bheema helped Draupadi have her revenge by bringing the jewel on Ashwathama's head.

She fell in the final journey for the dubious sin of loving Arjuna more than her other husbands. How can one blame her for loving one as good looking, skilful and virtuous, particularly when he alone had won her?

In her union with her five husbands she had five valiant sons: Prativindhya, Sutasoma, Srutakarma, Sataneek and Srutasen. They were respectively the sons of Yudhishthira, Bheema, Arjuna, Nakula and Sahadeva.

On their final journey, Draupadi was the first to fall. Bheema wanted to know the reason for this; Yudhishthira said, 'Draupadi showed favouritism towards Arjuna and thus she fell.'

At this time Draupadi was almost a hundred years old.

Dronacharya

He was probably the world's first test-tube baby. BHARADWAJ was filled with lust when he saw the apsara GHRITACHI bathing in the Ganga at Haridwar. He ejaculated into the water; the semen was kept in the pitcher. Drona was born from that pitcher.

Bhishma appointed Drona, who had with great skill taken out the princes' ball from a well, for training the princes.

Drona was excessively fond of ARJUNA. In order to crown Arjuna as the best archer he had wrongfully asked EKALAVYA to cut off his right thumb and give it to him as his teacher's dues. He taught Karna the use of weapons but not of divine weapons as KARNA was the son of a charioteer.

When his friend DHRUPAD insulted him, he used the help of the princes, led by Arjuna, to imprison Dhrupad. Later, Drona let him go. He had a son ASHWATHAMA by his wife KRIPI. He loved Ashwathama dearly; this weakness was used against Drona in the war. By KRISHNA's advice, Bheema killed an elephant called Ashwathama. YUDHISHTHIRA then said to Drona, 'Ashwathama has been killed,' and then mumbled, 'an elephant'. Drona dropped his arms. Dhristadyumna, Dhrupad's son, then beheaded Drona, thus taking revenge for his father's dishonour. The PANDAVAS would otherwise not have been able to kill Drona. But his favourite disciple Arjuna was not able to accept that his most respected teacher Drona was killed in this manner. He protested loudly.

Drona was involved in several wrongdoings, including the killing of the boy ABHIMANYU, making Ekalavya cut off his finger, stealing cows, rejecting Karna and watching silently as Draupadi was being humiliated. But the depth of his knowledge in the use of weapons and his love for Arjuna was beyond question.

The sweet teacher–student relationship between Drona and Arjuna is an interesting aspect of the *Mahabharata*. If the relationship between the teachers and students in contemporary times were similar the social fabric would have been markedly different; few Dronas or Arjunas are to be found now.

Druhya

Son of YAYATI.

Drumil

Another name for UGRASENA.

Durvasa (1)

YAYATI and DEVYANI's son.

Durvasa (2)

The son of Atri and ANUSUYA, he was an extremely short-tempered sage. He would curse everybody at the slightest provocation. KUNTI was able to invoke the gods to have children by Durvasa's blessing.

By Durvasa's curse, DUSHYANTA had forgotten SHAKUNTALA. By DURYODHANA's cunning, he once, with his ten thousand disciples, became the guest of the Pandavas when they were living in the forest. In answer to Draupadi's prayers, KRISHNA ate a bit of spinach and rice from the magic plate that Surya had given to Draupadi and immediately Durvasa and his disciples were satiated. He and his group fled. By Krishna's help, the PANDAVAS were rescued from Durvasa's curse.

Duryodhana

DHRITARASHTRA's oldest son by GANDHARI. He and BHEEMA were born on the same day. He was born as the incarnation of Kali. YUDHISHTHIRA would call him SUYODHANA in the hope that one day good sense with prevail upon him.

Ever since he was a child, Duryodhana was envious of the Pandavas, particularly of Bheema. He tried to poison Bheema to death but was unsuccessful.

His father's blind affection for him made him very arrogant. With his friend Karna, his brother DUSHASANA and his uncle SHAKUNI he was always conspiring to kill the Pandavas.

Duryodhana had his father's permission for all his misdeeds—trying to kill the PANDAVAS in the house of wax, adopting unfair means in dice and defeating them twice, and sending them away to the forest. The wise Gandhari understood her son; but although she could never bless him wholeheartedly, she wished him well.

Once, Duryodhana went to KRISHNA's house in Dwarka; Arjuna went after him. When Krishna awoke he saw Arjuna first because he was sitting at his feet. So he gave Arjuna the first right of refusal. When Arjuna asked for Krishna Duryodhana heaved a sigh of relief.

Duryodhana felt that Krishna's army of 10 crore soldiers, the NARAYANI SENA, were more valuable than Krishna himself.

Krishna and Duryodhana were related by marriage. Krishna's son Shamba had married Duryodhana's daughter Lakshmana.

When he went to steal King VIRATA's cows he was vanquished by the Pandavas. Once previously he was taken prisoner by the gandharva CHITRASENA but released by Yudhishthira's mercy.

The unkind, haughty Duryodhana's reply to the Pandavas' request for five villages was, 'I will not even give to the Pandavas the bit of earth that sticks to the edge of a needle, without war.'

Duryodhana did not trust anyone. At various times he expressed his lack of trust of BHISHMA, DRONA, VIDURA, and even KARNA.

Duryodhana and BHEEMA had learned the art of fighting with clubs from Balarama. They were equal competitors. He was also quite skilled at using other weapons. For a proud man like him, hiding in Lake Dwaipayan was an act of extreme cowardice.

Bheema broke Duryodhana's thigh to keep his own promise to avenge Draupadi's insult. Duryodhana had gestured lewdly to Draupadi by slapping his thigh. Balarama tried to protest by attacking Bheema but Krishna deterred Balarama. Balarama had always been more affectionate towards Duryodhana.

In the war of Kurukshetra, the balance was tipped in Duryodhana's favour. In a triumph of diplomacy, many kings fought for Duryodhana.

He lived for about seventy-two years.

Dushala

DHRITARASHTRA's daughter, born of GANDHARI, she was the youngest of Gandhari's one hundred and one children. She was the wife of Jayadratha and her son was Surath. There is little about Dushala in the *Mahabharata*.

Dushasana

DHRITARASHTRA's third son, born of GANDHARI. He was DURYODHANA's accomplice in all his misdeeds. His name befitted him. There was no end to the list of wrongdoings that Dushasana was involved in, including poisoning BHEEMA, trying to torch the PANDAVAS in the house of lacquer, defeating the Pandavas through trickery in dice and banishing them to the forest, going to witness their misery in the forest, and dragging Draupadi into an open court and trying to disrobe her. He was like his brother in every way. Bheema, to honour his promise, killed him in the war and washed his mouth with Dushasana's blood. Bheema told Gandhari that he only touched his lips to his blood but did not drink it.

Dushyanta

King of the PURU dynasty. He was out hunting deer when he saw Shakuntala at the sage Kanva's ashram and was enchanted by her beauty. Her father was then away from the ashram. They married by the gandharva method. SHAKUNTALA had one condition—her son would have to be king. When Shakuntala's son Bharat grew up, by the advice of the sage Kanva, Shakuntala went to the court of King Dushyanta.

But by Durvasa's curse, Dushyanta had forgotten Shakuntala. Sad and angry, Shakuntala was about to return to her father's house when a divine voice said, 'Bharat is Dushyanta's son.' Dushyanta then accepted Shakuntala and Bharat. Dushyanta's kingdom was called Bharatvarsha after his son's name.

Dwaipayan (1)

Maharshi Krishna Dwaipayan Vedvyas; see VYASDEVA.

Dwaipayan (2)

A famous lake near the KURUKSHETRA. When DURYODHANA realized that he was lost in Kurukshetra he hid here.

Dwaita Forest

A pristine forest on the banks of the Saraswati. During their stay in the forest, the Pandavas spent much time here.

Ekalavya

Son of Hiranayadhanu, the king of hunters. An unusually gifted archer, he had wanted to be DRONA's pupil but was rejected by him.

One day, the PANDAVAS went hunting for deer. Accompanying them was a loyal dog who began to bark when they entered the forest; when the dog returned, the princes found that a skilled archer had hit seven arrows in such a way that the dog could not bark; but he was not bleeding. The arrows had sealed his jaws together. Who was this unusually talented archer?

The princes went to satisfy their curiosity. They saw a forester practising archery in front of a clay statue of Drona; he had been distracted by the dog's barking and had punished him thus.

Miffed, ARJUNA asked Drona, 'Did you not say that there would be no one as skilled as me in archery in the three worlds? But I do not have the skill that EKALAVYA has!'

Drona came to Ekalavya and said, 'Cut off the thumb of your right hand and give it to me.' Ekalavya carried out this cruel order without hesitating. Everyone was surprised.

This incident shows the meanness of Drona and Arjuna. But it also points to Ekalavya's unquestioning respect for his teacher, his generosity and greatness.

Ekchakra

After narrowly escaping from the fire in the house of wax the PANDAVAS spent some time here; Bheema also killed the wicked demon Bak here.

Gandeeva

ARJUNA's bow and arrow, Brahma made it and gave it to Chandra. Varuna got it from Chandra. Agni asked Varuna for it and gave it to Arjuna during the burning of the KHANDAVA FOREST. When Yudhishthira was insulted in war, he asked Arjuna to throw away his GANDEEVA; Arjuna almost went to cut him to pieces. Arjuna had vowed that if anyone else insulted his Gandeeva, he would kill him. On the final journey, according to Agni's orders, Arjuna threw the Gandeeva and the special quiver into the waters as a sign of returning it to VARUNA.

Gandhari

The mother of the KAURAVAS and wife of DHRITARASHTRA; GANDHARI was the mother of DURYODHANA and his ninety-nine brothers and his one sister DUSHALA.

VYASDEVA had given a boon to Gandhari, 'May you be the mother of one hundred sons.' When Kunti gave birth to YUDHISHTHIRA, and Gandhari had not still given birth, she became impatient and tried to deliver prematurely; a ball of flesh, hard as iron, came out. By Vyasdeva's advice, the ball of flesh, kept in cold water, was made into a thousand pieces and kept in a hundred pitchers of 'ghee'. Slowly, Gandhari's ninety-nine sons were born. Dushala was born last of all. (On the same day, Bheema was born to Kunti).Vyasdeva's boon came true.

Gandhari's wisdom, sacrifice and greatness knew no parallel.

Ganga

BHISHMA's birth mother and wife of SHANTANU. After giving birth to seven consecutive sons she threw them into the GANGA. When she was about to throw the eighth son in the Ganga, Shantanu stopped her. He broke his promise to her in order to ask her for a justification for this unseemly act.

Ganga revealed the whole story to Shantanu. The curse-ridden eight Vasus were born to Ganga. So that they could return to heaven as soon as they were born, Ganga had adopted this means.

At Shantanu's request, Ganga kept the eighth Vasu DEVAVRATA with her, taught him and then returned him to Shantanu and took leave.

Ghatotkach

BHEEMA's son from HIRIMBA. He was huge, ugly and very powerful. His pitcher-like head (ghat means pitcher) did not have any hair (kach) so he was called Ghatotkach.

Whenever he was recalled he would come to help the Pandavas. Once he bore DRAUPADI on his back to the Gandhamadan mountain.

He fought fiercely in the Kurukshetra with a full regiment of rakshasha soldiers. Duryodhana realized that defeat was inevitable and he incited Karna to fight Ghatotkach. Karna had reserved the Vaijayanti weapon to kill Arjuna but he used it to kill Ghatotkach. When everyone in the Pandava camp had broken down at Ghatotkach's death, Krishna was happy because he knew that now Karna would no longer be able to kill Arjuna.

When Ghatotkach knew that he was about to die he inflated his body; when he fell a regiment of Kuru soldiers were crushed under his weight.

Ghritachi

A celestial apsara. The sage BHARADWAJ ejaculated when he saw this apsara; the semen was stored in a pitcher. DRONA was born in that pitcher.

Girivraja

JARASANDHA's capital and present-day Rajgir.

Gita

Included in the 'Episode of Bhishma', it consists of eighteen sections. The valuable advice given by Lord KRISHNA to the dejected ARJUNA in order to motivate him to fight in the battle of Kurukshetra is the essence of the Gita.

Because it includes seven hundred verses, the Gita is also called Saptasati. Sri Ramkrishna said that Gita was the reverse of tagi, meaning one who sacrifices.

Granthik

NAKULA's assumed name when the Pandavas lived in disguise.

Gurakesh

Another name for ARJUNA as he had conquered sleep.

Halayudh

Another name for BALARAMA.

Hanuman

A character in both the *Ramayana* and the *Mahabharata*. He was the son of Pavan and thus the older brother of BHEEMA. He was one of the ten immortals.

When Bheema was going to get a hundred-petalled lotus from a lake on Gandhamadan mountain to cater to Draupadi's fancy, Hanuman obstructed his way.

Bheema said, 'Let me pass.'

Hanuman said, 'No, I will not.'

Bheema said, 'Just as Hanuman jumped across the sea, I can also jump over you. But God is within everyone, so I will not jump.'

Hanuman said, 'Hanuman? Who is that?'

Bheema said, 'He is my older brother.'

Hanuman smirked and said, 'Very well! I am old now. You may move my tail and carry on.'

Bheema failed. Then he understood that this was no ordinary person. He wanted to find out who he was. When he found out, he asked his brother to show the gigantic form that he had taken while crossing the sea. When he saw the form he was most surprised; he paid his respects to his older brother.

Hanuman told him where to find the lotus. He also said, 'I have helped Rama. I will help you too. I will sit on the flag of Arjuna's chariot and make so much noise that the hearts of many will stop beating.' Because Hanuman sat on the chariot, Arjuna's chariot was called Kapidhwaj (kapi means monkey, dhwaj means flag).

Hastinapur

Capital of the KAURAVAS. A descendant of Bharat and a predecessor of Pandavas and Kauravas, Hasti, founded this kingdom; thus it was called Hastinapur.

Hastinapur was supposedly located east of Delhi, on the southern bank of the Ganga and near Meerut.

Hirimb

Brother-in-law of BHEEMA. A notorious rakshasha who devoured human flesh. When the PANDAVAS were escaping from the house of wax, they were stopped by this tree rakshasha.

Wanting to eat human flesh, Hirimb sent his sister Hirimba to catch them and bring them to him. Impressed by Bheema's looks, Hirimba went to them in the guise of a beautiful woman and revealed her brother's plan.

When his sister was delayed, Hirimb set off in search of her.

The Pandavas were deep in slumber. In order not to disturb their sleep Bheema took Hirimb off to a distance and beat him to death.

Later, in accordance with Kunti's advice, Bheema married HIRIMBA.

Hirimba

BHEEMA's wife. After killing her brother HIRIMB, Bheema was about to kill her. But listening to the advice of YUDHISHTHIRA and KUNTI, and to please Hirimba, he married her on condition that once they had a child he would leave Hirimba and live with his brothers. Bheema's son Ghatotkach was born to Hirimba.

Ila

Daughter of Vaivasat Manu. By Vishnu's boon, she earned masculinity and took the name Sadyumna. Because he entered the curse-stricken forest of Mahadeva, he was changed back into a woman. Vashishtha, Ila's priest, demanded a boon on Ila's behalf that enabled her to be a man for a month and a woman for a month.

Indra

The king of the gods, he fathered Arjuna.

To invoke Indra, Kunti used, at Pandu's request, the mantra taught to her by Durvasa. From their union Arjuna was born.

When Arjuna went to heaven to get some divine weapons, Indra welcomed his son warmly and taught him music, dance and archery.

To save Arjuna, Indra, dressed up as a Brahmin, begged Karna to part with his armour and earrings. In exchange Indra gave him the Vaijayanti weapon.

Indraprastha

YUDHISHTHIRA's capital, located near Delhi.

Iravan

The son of ARJUNA and ULUPI. On the eighth day of the KURUKSHETRA, he killed the six brothers of SHAKUNI and died in the hands of the demon Alambush. Ulupi was not married to Arjuna and so Arjuna was not the natural father, but the biological father of Iravan.

Janmejay

ARJUNA's grandson, he was the son of PARIKSHIT and MADRAVATI and husband of Vapushtama. His son was SATANEEK. ASHWAMEDHADATTA, the son of Sataneek was the last character in the *Mahabharata*.

Because he wound a snake around the sage Samik, his father was killed by snakebite. He performed the Sarpayagna (sarpa means snake). Many snakes were killed in the fire of the yagna. But his father's killer escaped with the help of Indra and Astik, the nephew of Vasuki, the king of serpents.

In order to save himself from the sin of killing a sage, he once heard the entire *Mahabharata* from Baishampayan.

Jarasandha

King of Magadh and son of Vrihadrath, his son-in-law was KANSA; Kansa had married his two daughters Asti and Prapti. His son was called Sahadeva.

Vrihadrath had no children. The great saint Chandakoushik gave him a mango and said that if he fed it to his wife, she would have an extraordinary son.

Vrihadrath divided the mango into two equal halves and fed it to both his wives. The wives gave birth to two children with half a body each. The midwives left the two half-bodies at the crematorium. When a female rakshasha put the two halves of the foetus together, the newborn baby came to life. He was called Jarasandha (jara means foetus or uterus).

Jarasandha tried to kill Krishna, the killer of his son-in-law, but he was unsuccessful. In order to kill the wicked Jarasandha, Krishna, Bheema and Arjuna went to him in disguise. Bheema and Jarasandha fought for a long time. Then, by Krishna's advice, Bheema caught hold of his legs and broke the strength he was born with. Thus Jarasandha was killed.

Jayadratha

The king of Sindhu, he was the husband of DURYODHANA's sister DUSHALA, the father of Surath and the son of Vriddhakshetra. He had tried to abduct Draupadi when the Pandavas were living in Kamyak forest and was beaten up by Bheema; Bheema scalped him and let him go.

Jayadratha meditated and prayed to Mahadeva in order to take revenge; Mahadeva gave him a boon that at least on one day he would be able to defeat any of the Pandavas except Arjuna. The beastly Jayadratha used this boon on the day of killing Abhimanyu. He was guarding the mouth of the wheel and no one could enter it. Susharma, the king of Trigarta, had kept Arjuna busy elsewhere. Arjuna vowed that he would kill Jayadratha the next day before sunset.

KRISHNA then covered the sky with illusory clouds; JAYADRATH thought that the sun had set and he came out of the formation in which he had been hiding. According to Krishna's advice, Arjuna cut Jayadratha's head and dropped the head on his father's lap. As soon as his father, coming out of meditation, threw Jayadratha's head on the ground, he was decapitated, in accordance with his own stipulation. Vriddhakshetra had said, 'Whoever drops Jayadratha's head to the ground will be beheaded.'

Kali

BHEEMA's other wife, she was the sister of SHALYA, the king of Madra. She was very beautiful. Bheema's son by her was called Sarvagata.

Kamgita

YUDHISHTHIRA was very depressed when BHISHMA's last rites were performed after his death. Then Sri KRISHNA had with Yudhishthira a discussion on morality which was called 'Kamgita.'

Kank

This was the name assumed by YUDHISHTHIRA during the PANDAVAS' one year of living in disguise in the court of King VIRATA.

Kansa

KRISHNA's maternal uncle. According to a prophecy, the eighth child born of Devaki would kill Kansa. One by one, Kansa killed seven sons of the imprisoned DEVAKI. The eighth child Krishna was cunningly exchanged with Yogmaya, a newborn baby born of NANDA. When Kansa went to kill her she vanished into thin air but not before she had said, 'The person who will kill you is growing in Gokula.' All Kansa's efforts to kill Krishna were in vain. Krishna later killed Kansa, and BALARAMA killed Kansa's eight brothers.

Karenumati

NAKULA's other wife, the daughter of SISUPALA, king of Chedi. She was the sister of DHRISTAKETU. She gave birth to a son, NIRMITRA.

Karna (Vasusena)

Born of KUNTI when she was still single, he was fathered by Surya; he had no mortal father. He was adopted by the charioteer Adhirath and his wife Radha.

He had a golden armour on him; he was therefore called Vasusena (vasu means gold). He was called Vrisha for his valour, his adherence to truth and his virtue. He was adopted by Radha and so he came to be called Radheya. He was born of Kunti and therefore he was called Kounteya.

According to some, Narakasura was reborn as Karna; as a consequence Karna and Arjuna were lifelong enemies. After he was born, Kunti, fearing a scandal, put him in an attractive box which she set afloat on the river Ashwa. The box floated along the Ashwa, then the rivers Charmambati, Yamuna and finally the Ganga where Radha and Adhirath were bathing. They picked up the baby and gave him a home.

Karna, the son of SURYA, was very good-looking indeed. Like his father, good looks and valour seemed to radiate from his body. He was almost ten- and-a-half-feet tall.

He learnt the art of using weapons from KRIPA and DRONA but when he wanted to learn to use the Brahmastra from Drona, Drona refused because Karna was the son of a charioteer. Drona was, in reality, afraid that Karna's skill might outdo Arjuna's. Karna subsequently began to nurture hatred for Arjuna. He vowed to do better than Arjuna in the use of Brahmastra and other divine weapons.

In the guise of a Brahmin, Karna learned the use of weapons from Parasurama. One day, Parasurama was sleeping with his head on the thigh of his favourite disciple. A leech pierced Karna's thigh from one end to another but rather than disturb his teacher's sleep, Karna tolerated the pain in silence.

When Parasurama woke up, he realized Karna's real identity. He cursed his pupil, saying, 'You have deceived your preceptor; when death comes calling you will forget the application of all the divine weapons.'

Once, while he was practising the use of weapons, Karna unwittingly killed a holy cow belonging to a Brahmin. The Brahmin cursed him, 'While you are at war with the person you are practising so hard to outdo, the wheels of your chariot will sink into the ground. Your opponent will take the opportunity to cut off your head.' At the exhibition of the princes' skills when Karna had wanted to battle with Arjuna, Kripa demanded to know his family background. Karna hung his head in shame. Duryodhana embraced Karna and crowned him king of the kingdom of Anga.

At her swayamvar, DRAUPADI did not want to garland the son of a charioteer. Karna never forgot that humiliation. At the Kuru court, in order to avenge his own insult, he called Draupadi a whore. Karna had vowed, 'Until I kill ARJUNA, I will not let anyone else wash my feet. I will not take meat or alcohol. I will not disappoint anyone who wants something from me.'

Surya had warned Karna about INDRA. Yet, to keep his promise, Karna gave Indra his natural armour and his earrings. Indra also gave him the powerful Vaijayanti weapon.

He had cut the armour from his body by his own hands and thus he was called Vaikartan (kartan means cutting). He cut the earrings from his ear and therefore he was called Karna (meaning ear).

When Krishna failed as a messenger of peace he went to Karna. He informed Karna of his actual identity and urged him to join the Pandavas. He said Karna would be king and the other five brothers would serve him. Draupadi would also accept Karna as her husband. But Karna did not concede.

Kunti had visited Karna. She confessed her true identity and expressed remorse for her actions. At that moment Surya revealed himself to underline the truth of Kunti's statement. He also said, 'Listen to your mother; you will benefit a lot.'

Grateful to Duryodhana and bound by a promise to him, Karna could only assure Kunti that five of her sons would remain alive. But only either Karna and Arjuna would remain alive; one would have to die.

BHISHMA could not tolerate the proud Karna. Karna had promised that as long as his grandfather was alive he would touch his weapons.

Karna was Duryodhana's source of strength and support. Karna also gave himself fully in order to express his gratitude to Duryodhana.

Karna was one of the seven warriors who encircled Abhimanyu and killed him. In order to kill Ghatotkach, Karna used up the Vaijayanti weapon which he had reserved for Arjuna. Krishna jumped up in joy because even if Ghatotkach was killed Arjuna had gained a 'life'. On the day of the fight with Arjuna, the curses of Parasurama and the fight were fulfilled. The brave Karna begged for mercy from Arjuna but to no avail. Krishna reminded Arjuna of the humiliation of Draupadi and the killing of Abhimanyu. That incited Arjuna and, forgetting all rules of war, he beheaded Karna.

Karna is the most controversial character in the *Mahabharata*. If one were to put aside his conceit and his pettiness in some instances he could have been the greatest character in the *Mahabharata*. He was truthful and charitable and his courage had no equal.

Karna's wife Padmavati bore him three sons, Krishnasen, Vrishaketu and CHITRASENA.

Karnik

The Brahmin minister of DHRITARASHTRA. His job was to speak against the Pandavas and to poison Dhritarashtra's mind against them.

Kaurava

The successors of KURU. By this logic PANDU and his sons were also Kauravas. But they felt more proud to name themselves after their father.

Keechak

Brother-in-law of King VIRATA. He was the brother of Queen SUDESHNA. The depraved KEECHAK insulted DRAUPADI during the PANDAVAS' year in disguise. Draupadi rejected his humiliating proposals. BHEEMA was able to kill him through trickery.

Khandava forest

A forest in the Khandavas. KRISHNA and ARJUNA helped Agni set fire to this forest when he was hungry and looking for food. Agni, in turn, gave them many weapons.

Kiddam

A sage who had taken the form of a deer to unite with a gazelle. PANDU unwittingly shot an arrow at the sage. He cursed Pandu, 'if you have intercourse with a woman you will die.' That is what happened. One day, when Pandu saw MADRI dressed beautifully, he lost his self-control. Notwithstanding Madri's objections he had intercourse with her and immediately Kiddam's curse was fulfilled. Pandu died.

Koumodoki

KRISHNA's club. Agni asked Varuna for this club and gave it to Krishna during the burning of the KHANDAVA FOREST.

Kripacharya

SHARADWAN saw the apsara Gyanpadi and, filled with lust, his body ejected seminal fluid; from that fluid a boy and a girl were born. SHANTANU took pity on them and picked up the two children and brought them home. The boy was called Kripa (meaning mercy) and the girl was called Kripi. Later DRONA married KRIPI. Kripa or Kripacharya was the teacher who taught the Kuru princes the art of using weapons.

Two mention-worthy misdeeds were the killing of ABHIMANYU and the killing of the PANDAVAS in their camp at the dead of night.

The Pandavas accepted him with respect at the end of the war. When they left on their final journey he was appointed the teacher for Parikshit.

He was one of the ten immortals.

Kripi

Wife of DRONA and daughter of the sage SHARADWAN, she was the sister of Kripacharya and mother of ASHWATHAMA. For more, see KRIPACHARYA.

Krishna

The eighth incarnation of Lord Vishnu. He was the life-force and the main protagonist of the *Mahabharata*. The source of strength of the PANDAVAS, we cannot imagine the *Mahabharata* without Krishna.

He was responsible for many heroic actions including the killing of Kansa, the serpent Kaliya, the rakshasha Putana, SISUPALA. He was the absolute favourite of the Pandavas especially ARJUNA and DRAUPADI.

During the disrobing of Draupadi and DURVASA's sudden arrival he had protected the Pandavas. He was Arjuna's charioteer during the Kurukshetra.

He was killed by a hunter according to GANDHARI's curse.

His father was VASUDEVA and his mother was DEVAKI. His adoptive father was NANDA and YASHODA was his adoptive mother. His maternal grandfather was Devak. KANSA was the son of Devak's brother Ugrasena. Kansa was not Krishna's own uncle but his mother's cousin. Kunti was his father's sister. At Devaki's wedding there was a prophecy that her eighth child would kill Kansa. Kansa was frightened when he heard the oracle. He imprisoned his sister Devaki and brother-in-law Vasudeva.

Cruelly, he killed Devaki's six children. By a miracle Vishnu sent the seventh child to Devaki's sister Rohini's womb. That child was born of Rohini and named Balarama.

Kansa did not come to know any of this. He thought Devaki had miscarried.

Devaki's eighth child Krishna was born in the month of Bhadra on the eighth day of the waning moon. Nanda's wife also gave birth to a daughter on the same day; the child was called YOGMAYA.

On that night of inclement weather, Vasudeva exchanged the two children following divine orders. By God's will no one knew of that exchange; the guards were fast asleep with the help of the powers that be. Seshnag showed the way and Yamuna cleared the way.

When Kansa was about to crush Yogmaya by throwing her to the ground, Yogmaya slipped from Kansa's hands and vanished into the sky. She warned Kansa, 'I am Yogmaya; the person who will kill you is being reared elsewhere. Your destroyer is growing up in Gokula.' Afraid, Kansa ordered the killing of all the children in Mathura but he could not touch Krishna.

Krishna and Balarama grew up together. After killing Putana and the serpent Kaliya, Krishna killed Kansa; Kansa's father Ugrasena was released from prison and made to sit on the throne of Mathura. The two brothers learned the Vedas from the saint Sandipani. After killing the sea monster Panchjan he got his conchshell Panchajanya.

Rukmini, the daughter of Bhishmak, the king of Vidarbha, was engaged to Sisupala, the king of Chedi. But Rukmini secretly loved Krishna. When Krishna learnt of this, he abducted Rukmini. Sisupala attacked Krishna, was completely routed in battle and he fled. Rukmini gave birth to ten sons including Pradyumna and a daughter named Charumati.

Other than Rukmini, Krishna had four chief wives, Jambavati, Sushila, Satyavama and Lakshmana. According to one opinion, other than these, Krishna had another sixteen thousand wives. In the *Mahabharata*, Krishna first appeared in Draupadi's swayamvar. He recognized his cousin Arjuna. The selfless love that grew between the cousins from the glance that was exchanged at the swayamvar is the main prop of the *Mahabharata* and has lent immense value to it.

At Krishna's suggestion and with his help, Arjuna abducted Krishna's sister SUBHADRA. By Krishna's manoeuvring, the wicked King Jarasandha of Magadha was killed by Bheema.

When Yudhishthira performed the Ashwamedha Yagna for Krishna as a means of showing his respect for him, Sisupala lashed out at Krishna using abusive language.

Krishna had promised his aunt, Sisupala's mother that he would forgive one hundred misdeeds of Sisupala. When he exceeded a hundred misdeeds, Krishna no longer forgave him and used the Sudarshan Chakra to behead him.

When the Pandavas lost the game of dice and were banished to the forest, Krishna met them there and gave them advice on many matters. Krishna promised Draupadi, 'I will do whatever I can for you, do not fret. You will reign as the queen, I promise.'

Once, when the Pandavas were in the forest, Durvasa came with ten thousand disciples to visit the Pandavas at their hut. This was of course a conspiracy hatched by Duryodhana. Everyone had finished eating and Draupadi, wondering what she would feed them and ever-loyal to Krishna, cried for help, 'Oh Keshava, rescue me.'

Keshava appeared. 'There is nothing but a bit of rice sticking to the edge of the plate.' Draupadi surrendered herself.

'That will suffice. Give it to me.' Jagannath was satisfied with one little bit. Durvasa and his other disciples were sated to the point of being uncomfortable. To keep his reputation intact, Durvasa ran away.

The day after the marriage of Abhimanyu and Uttara, there was an assembly at King Virata's house to discuss the Pandavas' getting back their kingdom. Krishna proposed that they send a messenger to Hastinapur. The messenger was supposed to say that half the kingdom needed to be returned to Yudhishthira. Everyone except Balarama agreed to this. Dhrupad's priest was sent as the envoy.

Duryodhana and Arjuna both came to have Krishna on their side. Krishna had been sleeping. Duryodhana came first. He sat near Krishna's head. Arjuna came later and sat near his feet.

Krishna said, 'When I opened my eyes I saw Arjuna first. He is also younger of the two so I shall give him first choice. Arjuna, you can either take me or my army, the NARAYANI SENA, the strength of which is ten crore people. I will not bear arms or participate in the war.'

Arjuna wanted Krishna. Duryodhana was secretly astonished at Arjuna's foolishness and returned satisfied to Hastinapur.

Krishna came to Hastinapur to make a final attempt at averting the war. He made an excellent speech.

Duryodhana said, 'As long as I live I will not even cede the bit of earth that sticks to the end of the needle to the Pandavas.'

Krishna used friendly as well as aggressive tactics to prevail over Duryodhana. Vidura, Bhishma, Drona and even Gandhari came out to open court to prevail over him but in vain.

Duryodhana, in contrast, wanted to imprison Krishna. Krishna revealed his true form. By Krishna's mercy even Dhritarashtra, born blind, could see his real form.

Krishna went to Karna to appeal to him to join the Pandavas. He revealed Karna's true identity to him. Karna humbly let him know that he was unable to comply with Krishna's request. Krishna returned empty-handed.

When the war was about to begin, Arjuna saw Bhishma, Drona, Kripacharya and the others on the opposite side and said to Krishna who was his charioteer, 'I do not want any kingdom; I will not fight. I do not want to win any kingdoms by killing.'

At this point, Krishna narrated the Gita to Arjuna; the Gita is the essence of the _Mahabharata_. Arjuna snapped out of his illusions and took up arms.

On the third day of the war, Krishna wanted to kill Bhishma who was engaged in a fierce battle; he forgot his promise and rushed forward with his Sudarshan Wheel. Bhishma, a great devotee of Krishna, was very happy at this. This happened again on the ninth day of the war.

According to Krishna's advice, the Pandavas found out from Bhishma himself how to defeat him. Krishna also put forward the idea of the half-truth that was used to kill Drona. Krishna's logic was that there was nothing wrong in telling lies to save one's life.

YUDHISHTHIRA returned to the Pandava camp, overpowered by Karna's attacks and humiliated. He called Arjuna and told him, 'Do not pride yourself on killing all your enemies yourself; throw your Gandeev away. It does not become you.' Arjuna rushed to kill Yudhishthira as he had vowed that he would kill anyone who belittled his Gandeev.

Krishna stopped Arjuna and reproached him. Then he advised, 'Why don't you reprimand Yudhishthira? Reprimanding an elder is the same as killing him.'

In repentance, Arjuna went to kill himself. Again Krishna's censure could be heard. He advised, 'Praise yourself in your own words. That is the same as killing yourself.'

These incidents underline Krishna's closeness to the Pandavas.

After Abhimanyu was killed, Arjuna vowed to kill Jayadratha the next day, before sunset. If he was not able to do it he would have sacrificed himself in the fire. He had impulsively promised to do something that was almost impossible without thinking of the pros and cons of it. This time also Madhusudan alias Krishna came to the rescue. He used his powers to cover the sun with clouds before sunset. Jayadratha, who was hiding in the impenetrable circle, came out, jumping with joy for he knew that Arjuna's death was now irrevocable. Krishna immediately dispelled the clouds; Arjuna killed the defenseless Jayadratha.

JAYADRATHA's father, VRIDDHAKSHETRA, had declared that anyone who caused his son's head to fall to the ground would have his own head severed from his body. Krishna knew of this boon and informed Arjuna. By Krishna's directions, Arjuna cut off Jayadratha's head and dropped it into the lap of his father who was deep in meditation outside the Kurukshetra. Vriddhakshetra was startled; he dropped the head to the ground and was beheaded himself by his own curse. Without Krishna's help and subterfuge, Arjuna would have had to die that day. And without Arjuna the Pandavas' victory would have been impossible.

On the day of Karna's killing, Krishna encouraged Arjuna constantly and reminded him of his promise to kill Karna. The wheels of Karna's chariot had sunk into the ground. Karna begged for a moment of respite from Arjuna. He said, 'This is correct; this is the ethic of warfare.' Krishna foresaw that there would not be another such opportunity for killing Karna. To incite Arjuna he said, 'Karna, now you are giving so much advice about morality and ethics. Where was all your sense of ethics when you tried to poison Bheema, disrobe Draupadi, kill the Pandavas in the fire, when you did not return the Pandavas' kingdom and killed the helpless boy Abhimanyu?

The words worked like magic. Arjuna did not hesitate to kill Karna.

One cannot imagine Arjuna participating in the war without Krishna.

When Duryodhana was hiding in Lake Dwaipayan, Yudhishthira told him, 'If you defeat any of us brothers in a club-fight we will accept you as the victor.'

Krishna asked Yudhishthira, 'Do you want to return to the forest? What if he wants to fight with anyone other than Bheema?'

But the proud Duryodhana did not take that opportunity. Again the Pandavas were saved.

When BHEEMA adopted unfair means and hit Duryodhana on the thigh, Balarama rushed to attack Bheema. Krishna saved him.

After the war, Krishna cried while consoling Dhritarashtra and Gandhari. Here we see a god behaving like a human being.

In the dead of night Ashwathama killed Dhristadyumna, Shikhandi and the five sons of Draupadi. Bheema rushed to attack Ashwathama. Chased by Bheema, Ashwathama threw the heavy-duty

Brahmasira missile. Arjuna, in return, threw the same missile. The attack and counter-attack of the two Brahmasira missiles caused a near-cataclysm. It was decided that Arjuna's Brahmasira would pull out the jewel from Ashwathama's head and Ashwathama's Brahmasira would kill Abhimanyu's child, and the only successor of the Pandavas, Parikshit, growing in Uttara's womb. But Krishna returned him to life.

Dhritarashtra wanted to embrace Bheema. Krishna anticipated the turn of events. An iron statue of Bheema was ready. Dhritarashtra put his arms round it and destroyed it. Krishna saved Bheema yet again.

Gandhari, who was turned to stone with grief, cursed Krishna, 'Krishna, if you wanted you could have stopped this disaster. I curse you—thirty-five years from now your dynasty too will be destroyed. You will roam about in the forest. You will die a sad death. The sky will resonate with the cries of the widows of the Yadu dynasty just as today the cries of the widows of the Kuru dynasty are being echoed.'

Krishna smiled a little and said, 'I know that this will happen.'

Krishna appeared in front of his great devotee Bhishma who was lying on the bed of arrows. He revealed his luminous self; Bhishma passed away in peace.

Krishna returned to Dwarka but came back for Yudhishthira's Ashwamedha Yagna. Just then Uttara gave birth to a stillborn son. Everyone was in tears. As decided, Krishna revived the baby boy Parikshit.

Thirty-five years after Gandhari's curse, when the Yadu dynasty was on its way to destruction and Balarama had given up his earthly form, Krishna, weighed down with sadness, was meditating under a tree. A hunter, mistaking him for a deer, shot an arrow. The arrow hit Krishna's heel; his days as a mortal incarnation were over and he went back into the form of Vishnu. He probably lived for a hundred and seven years.

There is no doubt that Krishna was the greatest character of the *Mahabharata*. He had himself revealed why he had taken human form:

'Whenever Dharma [or truth and morality] declines and adharma [or immorality] prevails, I manifest myself, O Arjuna.

I am born again and again in various ages to emancipate the good and destroy evil and for the establishment of Dharma [or morality and truth].'

Also, see DRAUPADI.

Krishna Dwaipayan Vedavyas

See VYASDEVA.

Kritavarma

King of the Bhoja dynasty. He, along with ASHWATHAMA and KRIPA, participated in the heartless killing of the Pandava warriors in the dead of the night. He was killed by Satyaki during the destruction of the Yadu dynasty.

Kunti

The birth mother of KARNA, YUDHISHTHIRA, BHEEMA and ARJUNA, she was the stepmother of NAKULA and SAHADEVA. She was the daughter of Surasen and Mahishi, VASUDEVA's sister, KRISHNA's aunt (father's sister) and maternal aunt of SISUPALA.

Kunti was very intelligent and humble.

Her actual name was Pritha. Surasen's cousin Kuntibhoj was childless. He asked his cousin for Pritha and reared her. She was called Kunti as she was the adopted daughter of Kuntibhoj.

By Durvasa's blessings, Kunti could invoke any god and have a child by that god.

One day, Kunti wanted to test the power of this mantra and so she invoked SURYA. Kunti was then a single girl but Surya was most persistent; he impregnated Kunti.

Kunti put the newborn baby in a box and let it float down the river. The baby was Karna. Pandu was sterile. In order to produce heirs for the dynasty, Pandu had insisted that Kunti call the gods. Thus Yudhishthira was born when Kunti called Dharma, Bheema was born when Kunti called Pavan and Arjuna was born when she called Indra. Pandu wanted more sons this way but Kunti did not agree. Madri learned the mantra from Kunti and invoked the ASWINI KUMARAS; she gave birth to twin sons. She subsequently forgot the mantra and asked Kunti for it again. Kunti, out of jealousy, did not teach it to her again. She was worried that if Madri had twins again, her sons might be stronger or more than Kunti's.

During the princes' display of strength and skill, Kunti, recognizing Karna by his armour and earrings, fainted.

Because of her careless comments Draupadi had to garland all the five brothers as her husbands. She also organized the killing of BAK at Ekchakra.

When the Pandavas were banished for thirteen years she lived in Vidura's house.

When DHRITARASHTRA and GANDHARI, irritated by Bheema's reproaches, decide to retire to the forest, KUNTI, VIDURA and SANJAY accompanied them.

One day Yudhishthira heard from Narad that Kunti, Dhritarashtra and Gandhari had sacrificed their lives in the forest fire during meditation. Narad got this news from Sanjay. Yudhishthira's heart broke when he heard the news.

Before the Kurukshetra, Kunti went to Karna to reveal her true identity and bring him back to the Pandavas, but she failed. Karna initially spoke to her sternly, but then respectectfully said that he was bound by gratitude to Duryodhana and therefore could not help the Pandavas. Having come with a heart full of hope, she returned empty-handed. She bore the pain silently. For fear of shame she could not tell the Pandavas about Karna.

Kuntibhoj

KUNTI was the adopted daughter of Kuntibhoj who did not have any children of his own. So he brought PRITHA, the daughter of Surasen, and brought her up.

Kuntihoj died fighting for the PANDAVAS in the battle of Kurukshetra.

Kurukshetra

The holy place Kurukshetra became the battlefield in the war between the KURUS and the PANDAVAS. It was previously called Samantapanchak. Parasurama had exterminated all Kshatriyas from the earth twenty-one times and built five lakes with their blood here. Then he prayed with this blood for the peace of the departed souls of his ancestors.

The ancestors of the Kuru dynasty got the boon that if one is killed here or meditates here one goes to heaven. That is why everyone who was killed in the Kurukshetra went to heaven.

Lakshmana (1)

KRISHNA's wife. Her other name was Kaikeyi.

Lakshmana (2)

Daughter of DURYODHANA, she was the wife of Krishna's son SHAMBA. When Shamba went to abduct her he was imprisoned by the Kauravas. Later, Balarama freed him and gave her to Shamba.

Madravati

Wife of PARIKSHIT, Madravati was the mother of Janmejay and daughter-in-law of ABHIMANYU and UTTARA.

Madri

PANDU's seond wife, she was the daughter of Artayan, king of Madra. She was the mother of Nakula and Sahadeva and sister of Shalya, king of Madra.

By the curse of the sage Kindam, Pandu was incapable of begetting children. Kunti had a boon from Durvasa whereby she could invoke any god to be the father of her child. When Kunti had three sons by that boon Madri pleaded with Pandu to ask Kunti to teach her the mantra.

Using the mantra that she learned from Kunti, Madri invoked the Aswini kumaras and had twin sons. She wanted to have more children but she forgot the mantra. So she asked Kunti but Kunti did not want to teach her the mantras again; perhaps she was envious (the co-wife had twin sons at one go) or she was afraid (in case Madri had more sons than she did).

One spring, seeing Madri dressed up beautifully, Pandu could not control himself. As soon as he united with her, the sage Kindam's curse came true and Pandu died.

Kunti blamed Madri for Pandu's death and wanted to die with him. Madri stopped her and said, 'The king lost his life because he was attracted to me. I should die with him; please bring up my sons like they were yours.' Saying this, Madri jumped into her husband's funeral pyre.

Manibhadra

Grandson of JAYADRATHA and DUSHALA, son of Surath. When ARJUNA went to the land of Sindhu with the horse of the Ashwamedha Yagna, Surath died of fear. Arjuna consoled his cousin DUSHALA and his grandson Manibhadra.

Matsya

The kingdom of VIRATA; according to some, Matsya is present-day Jaipur, while according to others it is the western area of Dholpur in Rajputana.

Matsyagandha

Another name for SATYAVATI.

Moy

Son of Diti, he was an artiste amongst the giants. KRISHNA and ARJUNA saved him during the fire at Khandava. To express his gratitude, he built, at Krishna's suggestion, an extraordinary palace for YUDHISHTHIRA. DURYODHANA burned with envy when he saw the magnificent edifice.

He wrote a book called 'Moymat' about the construction of buildings. Despite INDRA's opposition, he married the apsara Hema. Indra killed him by striking him with thunder.

Nahush

King of the Chandra dynasty and son of Aayu. By Agastya's curse Nahush became a python. He trapped Bheema when the Pandavas were living in the forest. YUDHISHTHIRA came in search of Bheema and found that he was caught by Nahush. Nahush asked Yudhishthira many difficult questions and when Yudhishthira answered them correctly he let Bheema go. As Agastya had said, the piety obtained by seeing Yudhishthira relieved him of his curse and he went back to heaven.

Nakula

Son of MADRI and PANDU but born of another man. He was born of one of the ASWINI KUMARAS; SAHADEVA was his twin brother. He was very handsome and he fell in the final journey because of his vanity.

Before he went to the forest, he smeared dust all over his body to prevent women from getting enchanted by his looks and professing their love to him.

At the palace of King VIRATA, he was called GRANTHIK and he looked after the stables. His code name, to be used amongst the Pandavas, was Jayatsen. He did not fare too well at the battle. He lost to Karna's son Vrishasena and fled.

After he became king, YUDHISHTHIRA gave Nakula the responsibility of looking after the staff and soldiers and of disbursing salaries.

He fell in the final journey for his vanity.

He was of a calm temperament, taciturn and faithful to his brothers.

He had two wives, DRAUPADI and Karenumati, the daughter of Sisupala.

Sataneek was his son by Draupadi and NIRMITRA was his son by Karenumati.

He lived for about one hundred and six years.

Nanda

KRISHNA's adoptive father who lived in Gokula. After Krishna was born, VASUDEVA, without anyone else's knowledge, exchanged Nanda's daughter YOGMAYA with Krishna. His wife Yashoda was devoted to Krishna. Nanda took Krishna to Vrindavan because he was afraid that Kansa would kill him. Nanda invited Kansa to a yagna and he was killed at that time. Krishna and Balarama went with Nanda to Mathura and killed Kansa there.

Nandini

VASHISHTH's wish-cow. The eight Vasus stole her and by Vashishth's curse had to be born on earth. Seven Vasus returned to heaven as soon as they were born but since the eighth Vasu Dyu was the brain behind this theft, he had to spend a long time on earth as BHISHMA.

Nara Narayan

Son of Dharma (truth) and Ahimsa (kindness). They were saints of a higher order. The gods sent many apsaras to disturb their meditation but to no avail. To teach the gods a lesson, Nara created URVASHI from his thigh; then he created thousands of apsaras. The gods were mortified. According to the _Vamana Purana_, in the Dwapar era, Nara was born as ARJUNA and Narayan was born as KRISHNA.

Narayani Sena

KRISHNA's own army, which was highly skilled and very powerful. DURYODHANA got ten crore soldiers from that army for the KURUKSHETRA. ARJUNA wanted KRISHNA on his side rather than the army.

Nirmitra

NAKULA's son with his wife KARENUMATI, wife of SISUPALA, king of CHEDI. He died in the battle of KURUKSHETRA.

Nivatakabacha

A line of demons belonging to the family of Sanghlad, son of Hiranyakashipu. ARJUNA killed them.

Panchajanya

KRISHNA's conchshell, made form the bones of the giant Panchjan who was killed by Krishna.

Panchal

The kingdom of DHRUPAD, covering Punjab and its adjoining areas.

Panchali

DRAUPADI's other name.

Pandavas

PANDU's sons bore the name of Pandava instead of KAURAVA, although as the successors of Kuru they were also technically Kauravas.

Pandu

The son of AMBALIKA and VICHITRAVIRYA but born of Vyasdeva after the death of Vichitravirya. When Ambalika saw Vyasdeva at the time of the union she turned pale with fear and thus she gave birth to a pale child, PANDU.

When the sage Kindam was, in the form of a deer, having sexual intercourse with a gazelle, Pandu had unwittingly pierced him with an arrow. Kindam cursed him, 'If you have intercourse with a woman, you will die.'

Pandu had two wives Kunti and Madri. But Pandu could not beget sons. So he urged Kunti to invoke the gods. Kunti, who had a boon from Durvasa, got Yudhishthira, Bheema and Arjuna as her children by invoking the gods. Madri also got twin sons, Nakula and Sahadeva, in the same way.

One day when they were alone, Pandu was sexually excited by the way Madri was dressed up; his lust brought his death. Pandu died by the curse of Kindam.

Parashar

The father of Vyasdeva, son of Shakti and Adrishyanti and grandson of Vashishtha. He was the creator of the *Parashar Samhita*.

He had a relationship with Satyavati when she was single and thus Vyasdeva was born. By his mercy, Satyavati got her virginity back and the smell of fish that had clung to her body disappeared. Instead, she acquired a musky smell.

Parikshit

The son of ABHIMANYU and UTTARA and father of JANMEJAY. While he was in Uttara's womb, he was killed by the weapon Brahmasira; he was stillborn at the time of the Ashwamedha Yagna. According to a previous condition, Krishna brought him back to life. When Yudhishthira left on his final journey he crowned Parikshit as the king and successor.

He had wound a snake around the neck of the sage Samik. Samik's son Sringi cursed him that Takshak would bite him to death. That is exactly as things happened.

Phalgun

Another name for ARJUNA.

Pourav

Dynasties that were born of PURU are Pouravs; so the KURUS and Pandavas are all Pouravs.

Prabir

Son of the king Niladhwaj and Jwala. When he blocked the progress of the horse of Yudhishthira's Ashwamedha Yagna, Arjuna battled with him and killed him. His wife Jana jumped into the fire, determined to kill Arjuna. She became an arrow in the quiver of Vabrubahana. Vabrubahana killed his father with that arrow.

Pradyumna

Son of KRISHNA and RUKMINI, his wife was Kukudamati and son Aniruddh. He was killed at the time of the destruction of the Yadu dynasty.

Pritha

Another name for KUNTI.

Prativindhya

Son of DRAUPADI and YUDHISHTHIRA, he was killed by ASHWATHAMA in the dead of the night in the PANDAVA camp.

Prishat

His other name is Bajjasen. He was the father of DHRUPAD, king of Panchal.

Purochan

DURYODHANA's trusted minister and architect. He built the house of wax at Varanavat where Duryodhana had planned to burn the Pandavas to death. Visura managed to send a digger and save the Pandavas. As fate would have it, Purochan died in a fire in his own house

Radheya

Another name for KARNA.

Rohini

BALARAMA's mother and VASUDEVA's wife, she was the daughter of Devak. After the destruction of the Yadava dynasty, she killed herself along with Vasudeva.

Rukmini

Wife of KRISHNA and daughter of Bhishmak. Krishna abducted her when he heard that she was being married to Sisupala. Krishna had ten sons including Pradyumna and one daughter, Charumati, by her.

Sabyasachi

Another name for ARJUNA.

Sahadeva

MADRI and PANDU's son, but born to another man. He was born of one of the ASWINI KUMARAS. NAKULA was his elder twin. He was very intelligent. His downfall in the final journey came as a result of his pride in his intelligence.

He kept his promise of killing SHAKUNI. KUNTI loved this son of Madri's. When they were banished to the forest, SAHADEVA blackened his face. He did not want to show his face to anyone.

Like Nakula, Sahadeva was an ordinary warrior. At King Virata's house, he took the name of Tantipala and looked after the cows. His code name to be used amongst the brothers was Jayadwal.

Sahadeva was even more aggressive than Bheema. When Krishna went to Hastina as a messenger to try and stop war, Bheema and Arjuna wanted to avert war. But Sahadeva and Draupadi wanted war. They did not want to extinguish the fire of revenge with pacifist sentiments. They wanted to express their desire for revenge.

Sahadeva killed Shakuni and his son Uluk but no other notable warrior.

On their final journey he fell because of his assumption that there was no one as intelligent as him.

Sahadeva had four wives: Draupadi, Vijaya, the daughter of the king of Madra, Bhanumati, and Jarasandha's daughter. He had two sons, Srutasen with Draupadi, and Suhotra with Vijaya. The names of the children born to Bhanumati and Jarasandha's daughter are not known.

By our estimation, Sahadeva lived for one hundred and six years.

Sairindhri

DRAUPADI's assumed name while she was in disguise.

Samantapanchak

An older name for KURUKSHETRA.

Sanjay

DHRITARASHTRA's big support, charioteer, friend and minister, he was the son of the charioteer Gabalpan. He tried to persuade Dhritarashtra to refrain from war, but he could not convince the father who blindly loved his son.

Vyasdeva had blessed Sanjay with divine sight. Sanjay gave an incredible commentary on the Kurukshetra. He was the world's first journalist. The objectivity of his narration is amazing. At the end of the war, Dhritarashtra, Gandhari, Kunti, Vidura and Sanjay retired to the forest. When Dhritarashtra and the others died in the forest fire, Sanjay, according to Vyasdeva's suggestion, went to the Himalayas and left his earthly body while meditating.

Sanjay was one of the best characters of the _Mahabharata_. The dutifulness of this minister and charioteer who was enlightened about the three worlds was unparalleled.

Sankarshan

Another name for BALARAMA.

Sarbaga

BHEEMA's son, born of Kashiraj's daughter Balandhara. He died in the KURUKSHETRA.

Sarmistha

Wife of Yayati, she was the daughter of Vrishaparba, the king of asuras. She had three sons—Druhya, Anu and Puru. The Pouravs were the descendants of Puru. By this logic, the PANDAVAS and the KAURAVAS are all Pouravs.

See DEVYANI for more.

Sarvagata

BHEEMA's son by Kali, sister of SHALYA, king of Madra. He died in the battle of KURUKSHETRA.

Sataneek

Son of DRAUPADI and NAKULA. He was killed by ASHWATHAMA when he raided the PANDAVA camp in the dead of night.

Satyabrata

BHISHMA's other name.

Satyaki

King of the Yadu dynasty, he was the son of Satyaka and grandson of Shini. He was also known as Yuyudhan. He was Krishna's charioteer and ARJUNA's disciple.

In the assembly of peace envoys after ABHIMANYU's wedding, Balarama criticized Yudhishthira harshly. Satyaki protested; he wanted war. When Bhurisraba, to keep his promise, hit him with his foot, Satyaki killed him by using unfair means.

He did not support the killing of Drona. He went to attack DHRISTADYUMNA. When the Yadu dynasty was being destroyed,

Satyaki, in a state of excitement, attacked Kripavarma. Bhoja and Andhakara used huge plates to attack and kill Satyaki. Krishna's son Pradyumna tried to rescue Satyaki but was killed.

Satyavati

Shantanu's wife and mother of CHITRANGAD and VICHITRAVIRYA, she was BHISHMA's stepmother. VYASDEVA was born to her outside wedlock.

Uparichay, the king of Chedi, had gone deer hunting when he remembered his beautiful wife Girika. He became so excited that he ejaculated; the semen was sent by a hawk to his wife. This hawk was attacked by another and the semen fell into the waters of the Yamuna.

An apsara, Adrika, lived in the water as a fish. Adrika swallowed the semen and ten months from then she was caught in a fisherman's net.

When the fisherman cut the fish, he found two children—a boy and a girl. Adrika was relieved of her curse.

The fisherman called the boy Matsya and the girl SATYAVATI. Satyavati smelt of fish and thus she was also called Matsyagandha (matsya means fish and gandha means smell).

The young girl Matsyagandha used to ferry her boat across the river. One day Parashar got on her boat and fell in love with her. He manufactured mist in the middle of the river and united with Satyavati. Not even the birds sensed anything.

On an island, Satyavati gave birth to a boy with a very dark complexion; the boy was Krishna Dwaipayan Vedavyas.

By Parashar's mercy, Satyavati got back her virginity. The smell of fish vanished from her body. Instead, her fragrance wafted into the distance. Matsyagandha became Yojangandha (yojan is a measure of distance and gandha means smell).

Shantanu fell in love with Satyavati and wanted to marry her. Satyavati's adopted father had one condition: Satyavati's son would have to be made king. Shantanu and Satyavati's marriage was enabled by Bhishma's two vows. When her two sons died untimely deaths, Vyasdeva, her other son, impregnated her daughters-in-law. Satyavati had asked Bhishma to perform this duty. But Bhishma did not want to break his vow or his monastic way of life.

Before the war began, Satyavati, following Vyasdeva's advice, went to the forest and meditated. There she passed away.

Saubali

A Vaishya maid and mother of YUYUTSU. When GANDHARI was pregnant, SAUBALI took care of DHRITARASHTRA; Dhritarashtra's virtuous son YUYUTSU was born to her. There is not much about her in the _Mahabharata_.

Shakuni

King of Gandhar, he was Duryodhana's maternal uncle, Gandhari's brother, son of Subal and father of Uluk. He was vile and conniving. He was at the helm of all Duryodhana's misdeeds including trying to poison Bheema, trying to torch the Pandavas in a house of wax and looting Yudhishthira by cheating in the game of dice.

He beat Yudhishthira in dice, through trickery, not once but twice. He was killed by Sahadeva in the war.

Shakuni's brothers were Gabaksha, Sharabh, Vibhu, Subhag, Bhanudutt, Vrishak and Achal.

Shakuntala

Indra was anxious about Viswamitra's deep meditation. His fear was that Viswamitra would become more powerful than Indra. So he sent Menaka, a dancer of heaven, to disrupt Viswamitra's meditation. Viswamitra was enticed by the naked body of Menaka; Menaka gave birth to a daughter.

When Viswamitra returned to his penance, Menaka returned to Indra's court leaving the baby on the bank of the river Malini.

The great sage Kanva saw that a vulture had spread its wings and was protecting an abandoned, newborn baby. He brought her to his hermitage. Because she was protected by a vulture she was called Shakuntala (shakun is vulture). Shakuntala was reared affectionately by the sage.

Shalva (1)

Amba's lover. After Bhishma abducted Amba, Ambika and Ambalika, he learned that Amba loved Shalva. The broad-minded Bhishma let Amba go free. But since Bhishma had abducted her, Shalva rejected Amba. Shalva, in his previous birth, was Ajak, the son of Vrishaparba.

Shalva (2)

Sisupala's friend who was very angry when Krishna killed Sisupala. He vowed, 'I will free the world of Yadavas.' He attacked Dwarka.

Using an aircraft-like vehicle called Souva, he fought fiercely with Krishna. Krishna used the Sudarshan Chakra to kill Shalva and destroy his aircraft. The description of a fighter plane in the *Mahabharata* is surprising.

Shalva (3)

He fought for the KAURAVAS in KURUKSHETRA. DHRISTADYUMNA's elephant killed him.

Shalya

King of Madra and maternal uncle of the PANDAVAS. Brother of MADRI. When he was on his way to join the PANDAVAS, DURYODHANA craftily won him over to his side. In the name of being KARNA's charioteer, he provoked Karna and covertly helped the Pandavas. He was killed by YUDHISHTHIRA on the last day of the war.

Shamba

KRISHNA's son, born of Jambavati.

Shamba abducted DURYODHANA's daughter Lakshmana from her swayamvar. The KAURAVAS took him prisoner. BALARAMA was very fond of Shamba. He rescued Shamba from the Kauravas and organized his marriage with Lakshmana. Once, Viswamitra, Kanva and Narad had come to Dwarka. Shamba and his Yadava friends wanted to have some fun at the expense of the sages. The friends dressed Shamba as a pregnant woman and took him to the sages and asked whether a girl or a boy would be born. The sages were very angry. They cursed, 'He will give birth to a mallet which will destroy the Yadu dynasty.'

The words of the sages were not to be proved wrong; the next day, Shamba gave birth to a mallet. It was quickly thrown into the sea. But with time, a forest was made from the grass growing on it. The Yadavas fought amongst themselves with those trees and brought about their own end.

Shantanu

Husband of GANGA and SATYAVATI and son of Pratip. He was the father of BHISHMA, CHITRANGAD and VICHITRAVIRYA.

Shantanu was mesmerized when he saw Ganga and wanted to marry her. Ganga had one condition—he would not question any of her actions. If he did, she would return to heaven.

One by one, Ganga sacrificed Shantanu's seven children into the river as soon as they were born. Shantanu, bound by his promise, tolerated her inhuman actions silently; if he said anything, she would return. When the eighth child was born, Shantanu could not control himself any longer. He stood in her way and demanded to know the reason for her actions. Ganga said, 'I will give an explanation but I will also go away.'

Ganga revealed the true identity of her eight sons. She took the eighth child and left. After thirty-six years, when he had attained the highest form of learning, she returned him to his father. The child became Bhishma.

Shantanu had also wanted to marry Satyavati, the daughter of Dasraj; Dasraj had a condition—Satyavati's son would have to be crowned king.

Shantanu was dejected as he did not want to marry at the cost of depriving Bhishma of his right to be king.

Bhishma heard the conditions and made two promises: one that he would not become king, and two that he would not marry. Shantanu blessed Bhishma saying that he would die by his own wish. Devavrata became Bhishma.

Shantanu and Satyavati got married. They had two sons, Chitrangad and Vichitravirya. But by a cruel twist of fate, Satyavati's sons could not carry on the family lineage. They died young.

Sharabh

SISUPALA's son who had stopped the horse of the Ashwamedha Yagna. ARJUNA forced him to accept the suzerainty of YUDHISHTHIRA.

Sharadwan

He was a disciple of the great saint Gautama. On seeing the apsara Gyanpadi, he was filled with lust. His semen fell on an arrow and was split into two parts. Two children, KRIPA and KRIPI were born from the two parts. He is best known as Kripacharya's father and as DRONA's father-in-law.

Shikhandi

SHIKHANDI was the son of DHRUPAD, DRAUPADI's father and the brother-in-law of the PANDAVAS.

Rejected by BHISHMA, AMBA sacrificed herself in the fire saying that she would be the reason for Bhishma's death in her next life. Later, by Mahadeva's boon, she was born in Dhrupad's family as his daughter. According to Mahadeva's boon, the girl would later turn into a boy. Dhrupad announced that he had had a son. He married Shikhandi to Hiranayavarma's daughter.

Hiranayvarma came to know of Dhrupad's deceit from his daughter. He declared war against Dhrupad.

Shikhandi went to kill herself in the forest. The yaksha Sthunakarna lent her his masculinity for a while. After fighting on behalf of his father, Shikhandi came to Sthunakarna to return his loan. Sthunakarna's lord, Kuber heard the story and cursed that Shikhandi would remain a man and Sthunakarna a woman. This would not change in Shikhandi's lifetime.

Bhishma knew all of this. When the Pandavas could not outwit Bhishma in any way in the Kurukshetra, by Krishna's advice they went to ask Bhishma himself ways and means to defeat him. Remembering Amba's pledge, Bhishma hinted that if he saw Shikhandi on Arjuna's chariot, he would put down his arms. As per the advice, Arjuna sat Shikhandi in front of his chariot and attacked Bhishma with a volley of arrows.

Ashwathama killed Shikhandi in the dead of night in the Pandava camp.

Sisupala

King of CHEDI and of the Vrishi dynasty. Son of Dum and SRUTASRABA, he was KUNTI's sister's son and KRISHNA's cousin, father of SHARABH and DHRISTAKETU and father-in-law of NAKULA.

Narayana's gatekeeper Jay was born as Hiranakshya in the Satya era, Ravana in Treta and Sisupala in Dwapar era.

He was born with three eyes and four hands and brayed like a donkey. A divine prophecy predicted that his extra eye and hands would come off when he was in the lap of a person but that person would be his killer. His parents were afraid.

Once, when Krishna had come to visit his aunt, he took him in his lap; as soon as he did this, the additional eye and hands came off. The child's mother screamed—her nephew would kill her son! Krishna promised Srutasraba that he would forgive one hundred faults of Sisupala's. When Sisupala grew up and came to know of this prophecy, he hated Krishna from the core of his heart.

When Sisupala's marriage was fixed with Rukmini, Krishna abducted Rukmini. Sisupala's anger was fuelled.

The best reward of Yudhishthira's Rajasuya Yagna was given to Krishna at Bhishma's suggestion. Incensed, Sisupala abused Krishna and Bhishma in vile language.

Krishna lost his patience. He said, 'I had promised his mother that I would forgive a hundred wrongs done by him. Today he has exceeded one hundred. I will not forgive him any longer.' Saying this, he used the Sudarshan Chakra to behead Sisupala.

Somdatta

Son of Bahlik, a king of the Kuru dynasty. Bhurisraba's father. He joined the Kauravas in the battle of KURUKSHETRA. He was killed by Satyaki on the fourteenth day of battle.

Soubal

Another name for SHAKUNI.

Sounak

A great saint who had meditated for twelve years.

Souti

He was the narrator of the Puranas. A Suta, he was the son of Lomharshan. He heard the *Mahabharata* from Vaishampayan at the

Snake Yagna of Janmejay. He later recited it to Sounak and his sages at the Naimish forest.

Sringi

Son of the sage Samik. One day, PARIKSHIT wound a dead snake around Samik's neck. Sringi cursed Parikshit 'Within ten days, you will be killed by Takshak biting you.' That is what happened.

Srutakarma

Son of ARJUNA and DRAUPADI, he was killed by ASHWATHAMA in the dead of night in the PANDAVA camp.

Srutasen

Son of SAHADEVA and DRAUPADI, he was killed by ASHWATHAMA in the dead of night in the Pandava camp.

Srutasraba

She was the mother of SISUPALA, sister of KUNTI and VASUDEVA, daughter of SURASEN and MAHISHI, wife of the king of CHEDI. She was also Krishna's aunt.

Sthunakarna

When SHIKHANDI married Hiranayavarma's daughter, it became known that Shikhandi was not a man but a woman. Hiranayavarma, shocked at DHRUPAD's deceit, declared war. When Shikhandi went to the forest to kill herself, Kuber's follower Sthunakarna lent her his masculinity. At the end of the war, Shikhandi came to return her loan but by Kuber's curse, Sthunakarna remained a woman and Shikhandi a man.

Subal

King of Gandhar, he was the father of GANDHARI and SHAKUNI, father-in-law of DHRITARASHTRA, grandfather of DURYODHANA and ULUK. Other than Shakuni, Subal had seven sons: Gabaksha, Sharabh, Vibhu, Subhag, Bhanudutt, Vrishak and Achal.

Subhadra

ARJUNA's wife and sister of KRISHNA and BALARAMA, she was the daughter of VASUDEVA and ROHINI.

Arjuna was captivated when he saw Subhadra at the Raibatak mountains. With Krishna's help, Arjuna abducted Subhadra. Balarama was upset. Krishna pacified him. At Satyavama's enthusiasm, their wedding was organized in Dwarka.

Subhadra was stunningly beautiful. Even in her old age, her complexion was like gold.

During the war, Subhadra and Draupadi stayed in the Pandava camp. When they left on their final journey, Arjuna left Subhadra in the care of their grandson Parikshit.

She was able to see the dead Abhimanyu once, by Vyasdeva's mercy.

Sudeshna

Queen of King VIRATA, she was the mother of UTTAR and UTTARA, sister of Keechak and Abhimanyu's mother-in-law. When the Pandavas were living in disguise, Draupadi, as Sairindhri, worked as her maid for one year.

Suhotra

Son of SAHADEVA and Vijaya, daughter of SHALYA, king of MADRA. He died in the battle of Kurukshetra.

Sukdev

VYASDEVA was so filled with lust when he saw the apsara GHRITACHI that his semen fell out and on to the wood used for lighting the fire for a holy yagna. Ghritachi was frightened and flew off in the form of a parrot. Vyasdeva rubbed one piece of wood against the other and fire was lit. A beautiful child emanated from the fire; the child was Sukdev. As Ghritachi had flown off as a parrot, he was called Sukdev (suk means parrot).

Ganga came herself and bathed the child. Mahadeva put the sacred thread on him. Indra gave him divine weapons and a holy water-pot. His teachers were Vrihaspati, Vyasdeva, Janak and Narad.

Sukdev had conquered lust to the extent that he remained unaffected when apsaras were naked in front of him. He attained enlightenment on the strength of his meditation. He was more knowledgeable than Vyasdeva.

Surasen

KRISHNA's grandfather; father of VASUDEVA, KUNTI and SRUTASRABA. His wife was Mahishi. He gave his daughter Pritha (or Kunti) to his cousin Kuntibhoj to adopt. Kuntibhoj named her Kunti.

Surath

Son of JAYADRATHA. When he heard that ARJUNA had come to Sindhu with the horse of the Ashwamedha Yagna, he died from fear.

Surya

A god of the Hindu pantheon. The son of Kashyap and Aditi, he was also called Aditya.

KUNTI, young and single, wanted to test the power of the mantra given to her by Durvasa; out of curiosity she called Surya. Immediately, Surya appeared. Kunti asked him to go back as she was single but he was persistent; Kunti subsequently gave birth to Karna. To save herself from scandal, Kunti floated Karna on the river Ashwa.

Surya helped his son at every step. When Arjuna's birth-father Indra came to take Karna's armour and earrings, Surya conveyed this news to KARNA. Karna of course did not go back on his vow.

Susharma

King of Trigarta and friend of DURYODHANA.

King VIRATA and Keechak once attacked Susharma's kingdom. When Keechak was killed, he attacked the kingdom of Matsya with Duryodhana's help. Virata was taken prisoner. By Yudhishthira's orders, Bheema secured Virata's release and kicked Susharma. Yudhishthira let Susharma go.

As per plan, Susharma kept Arjuna busy elsewhere on the battlefield on the day Abhimanyu was killed. The main objective was that Arjuna should not enter the circular formation battle-order. When Abhimanyu died, Arjuna killed Susharma in anger.

Suta

If a Kshatriya impregnated a Brahmin woman, the child was called a Suta. Sutas usually worked as charioteers.

Sutasoma

Son of BHEEMA and DRAUPADI, he was killed by ASHWATHAMA in the dead of night.

Suyodhana

YUDHISHTHIRA called DURYODHANA by this name. See DURYODHANA.

Takshak

One of the main eight snakes; his other name was Anantnag. He was the brother of Vasuki.

Krishna and Arjuna set fire to the Khandava forest to help Agni assuage his hunger. Takshak's wife and son were killed by Arjuna's arrows while they were trying to escape. Parikshit put a dead snake around the neck of the sage Samik. Samik's son Sringi cursed him saying that he would die of snakebite within seven nights;

subsequent events took that course. Takshak took his revenge for the death of his son and wife.

Tantipala

SAHADEVA's assumed name during the Pandavas' stay in disguise.

Tara

Tara was the wife of Vrihaspati, the teacher of the gods. Chandra (the moon) abducted her, captivated by her beauty. Budh (or Mars) was born to Tara. Vrihaspati got back Tara with Brahma's help.

Ugrasena

King of the Yadu dynasty, he was the son of Ahuk and Kashya, father of KANSA and brother of Devak, the maternal grandfather of KRISHNA. Kansa had imprisoned him. When Krishna and Balarama killed Kansa they released him and he was made to sit on the throne.

Uluk

DURYODHANA's messenger to the PANDAVAS, he was the son of SHAKUNI and Duryodhana's cousin. He had unhesitatingly delivered Duryodhana's message causing a great stir. He was killed by Sahadeva on the eighteenth day of the battle. Sahadeva had vowed to kill Shakuni and Uluk.

Ulupi

Daughter of the king of serpents. One day, while ARJUNA was bathing in the Ganga, Ulupi caught a hold of him and pulled him away to the underworld. Ulupi, although married, wanted to marry Arjuna but Arjuna did not agree. But at Ulupi's insistence they spent a night together and Iravan was born. When Vabrubahana shot Arjuna with his arrow, Ulupi got the life-giving nectar from the underworld.

When the Pandavas left on their final journey Ulupi went back to the Ganga.

Upakeechak

King VIRATA's brother-in-law and brother of KEECHAK. There were one hundred and five Upakeechaks. They took Draupadi with them to the crematorium to burn her body along with that of Keechak. They were killed by Bheema who heard Draupadi's cries and rushed to save her.

Upaplavya

A city in the kingdom of King VIRATA. At the end of their year of living in disguise, the Pandavas organized the battle from here.

Urvashi

A celestial apsara or angel. There are different stories about her birth. Some say that she was born of Narayana's thigh or that she was born when the oceans were churned. Some think that the seven Manus together created her.

Urvashi had looked, mesmerized, at Pururba while she was dancing, causing a break in the rhythm. Indra cursed her to be born as a mortal. She married Pururba. The gandharvas then conspired to get her back to heaven.

Although Urvashi returned to heaven, she agreed to meet him once every year. Thus she gave birth to seven sons by Pururba. Later, by the gandharvas' boon Pururba and Urvashi were able to live in heaven.

ARJUNA had learned dance and music from the gandharva Chitrasena. Urvashi wanted to be with Arjuna but Arjuna rejected her with great humility. He said, 'I respect you like my mother.' Urvashi was the mother of Aayu, the grandfather of Puru, one of the first men in Arjuna's dynasty. By Urvashi's curse, Arjuna was to lose his masculinity. This helped Arjuna when he had to disguise himself as Vrihannala.

Uttamouja

Son of DHRUPAD and brother of DRAUPADI, he was a great warrior. At the end of the war, Ashwathama killed him, along with many others, in the dead of night.

Uttar

Son of King VIRATA, he was also known as Bhuminjay. When Duryodhana and his cohorts came to steal cows from King Virata, Prince UTTAR went to battle with great flourish, taking VRIHANNALA as his charioteer. During the battle, Uttar wanted to flee and Arjuna made him act as his charioteer. Vrihannala revealed himself as Arjuna and fought a fierce battle.

A simple soul, Uttar was killed on the first day of the KURUKSHETRA by SHALYA, the maternal uncle of the Pandavas.

Uttara

Daughter of King VIRATA and Queen SUDESHNA. She was the wife of Abhimanyu. As VRIHANNALA, ARJUNA taught her music and dance. She was carrying Parikshit in her womb when Abhimanyu was killed. The Brahmasira weapon shot by ASHWATHAMA killed the child in her womb, When she gave birth to a dead child during the Ashwamedha Yagna everyone was very upset. But as had been decided, Krishna revived the baby. That baby was Parikshit.

Vaan

Son of Bali, the king of demons. His daughter Usha married KRISHNA's son Aniruddh.

Vabrubahana

Son of ARJUNA and CHITRANGADA, king of Manipur. When he stopped the horse of the Ashwamedha Yagna, he and Arjuna were locked in a fierce battle. Jana, Prabir's wife, had vowed to kill Arjuna in her next life. She took refuge as Vabrubahana's arrow and killed Arjuna. Because of Chitrangada's tears, Ulupi came from the netherworld and revived Arjuna.

Vallabh

BHEEMA's assumed name while staying at King Virata's palace in disguise.

Varanavat

Present-day Prayag where the Kauravas hatched the conspiracy of torching the Pandavas to death in a house of wax but failed. VIDURA sent a digger who dug a tunnel through which the PANDAVAS and KUNTI escaped. When BHEEMA himself set fire to the house of wax, a hunter and his five sons died. The Pandavas were saved.

Varuna

He was the other main god. At the time of setting fire to Khandava, Agni took weapons from Varuna and gave them to Arjuna and Krishna. He gave Arjuna two quivers with unlimited capacity, the Gandeev and a chariot with a flag carrying the insignia of a monkey. He gave Krishna the Sudarshan Chakra and the Koumodoki club.

Vasudeva

KRISHNA's father, he was the son of Surasen and Mahishi, brother of Kunti and Srutasraba and maternal uncle of Sisupala. He married the seven daughters of Devak including Devaki and Rohini. Krishna was born to Devaki and Balarama and Subhadra were born to Rohini.

He was imprisoned for a long time in Kansa's jail. He left his earthly body while meditating after the death of Krishna and Balarama and after communicating Krishna's final instructions to Arjuna.

Vasuki

King of serpents. He sent his nephew Asteek to rescue his brother Takshak from the Snake Yagna of Janmejay.

Vichitravirya

Son of SHANTANU and SATYAVATI and brother of CHITRANGAD, he was the father of PANDU and DHRITARASHTRA although he did not give birth to them. He had two wives, AMBA and AMBALIKA. Indulgence in earthly and sensual pleasures caused his early death. He died without any children.

Vidura

The son of the great saint KRISHNA DWAIPAYAN VYASA and a slave woman in the royal palace. By the curse of the sage, Animandavya, Dharma was reborn as Vidura. Since Dhritarashtra was blind from birth, SATYAVATI asked AMBIKA to have intercourse with Vyasdeva again. Thinking about Vyasdeva's monstrous looks, Ambika was scared and she sent her maid in her place. That maid gave birth to Vidura.

Vyasdeva had told the maid, 'Your offspring will be the most clever and virtuous.' Vyasa's words were never wrong. Vidura's wife Devika gave birth to a few sons but their names are not known. Vidura was very fond of the Pandavas. He rebuked Dhritarashtra and Duryodhana for every misdeed of theirs but to no avail.

When the PANDAVAS were banished to the forest, Kunti spent those thirteen years with Vidura. Vidura sent a digger to save the Pandavas from being burnt to death in the house of wax.

When DHRITARASHTRA and GANDHARI retired to the forest, Vidura went with them. When Yudhishthira heard that Vidura was a little mentally disturbed in the forest, he went to see him. Dharma left Vidura's body and entered Yudhishthira's. There was an oracle forbidding the cremation of Vidura's body. Yudhishthira's moral strength was consolidated when Dharma took shelter in his body.

Vijay

Another name for ARJUNA.

Vijaya

SAHADEVA's other wife, daughter of SHALYA, King of Madra. In her swayamvar, Vijaya garlanded her cousin Sahadeva. She and Sahadeva gave birth to a son Suhotra.

Vikarna

DHRITARASHTRA's son by GANDHARI. Honest and virtuous. When Draupadi was being humiliated in the court, only he had protested openly. It was his misfortune that he had to take up arms against the Pandavas. Bheema, bound by his promise, killed him.

Virata

The king of Matsya. His wife was SUDESHNA, his sons were Sankhya and Uttar, and his daughter was UTTARA. Uttara and ABHIMANYU were married. His brother was SATANEEK and brother-in-law was KEECHAK. The five Pandavas and Draupadi stayed in his palace, in his shelter, using assumed names. He was killed by Drona on the fifteenth day of the KURUKSHETRA.

Vibhatsu

Another name for ARJUNA.

Vrikodara

Another name for BHEEMA.

Vrishaketu

Son of KARNA and PADMAVATI. KRISHNA, in the guise of a hungry Brahmin, wanted to eat the flesh of Vrishaketu. Padmavati, in tears, cooked the meat. Krishna was impressed with Karna's commitment to truth and hospitability. He revived Vrishaketu. After the Kurukshetra, his Pandava uncles welcomed him warmly.

Vrihadashwa

A sage who narrated the story of Nal and Damayanti to YUDHISHTHIRA and taught him the Akshahriday lesson.

Vrihannala

ARJUNA's assumed name when they were living in disguise.

Vedavyas

Another name for VYASDEVA.

Vaikartan

Another name for KARNA.

Vaishampayan

A disciple of VYASDEVA. He had narrated the *Mahabharata* to JANMEJAY.

Vyasdeva
(Maharshi Krishna Dwaipayan Vedavyas)

The composer of the *Mahabharata*. Vedavyas was also the writer of *Puranprakashak*, *Mahabharata* and the Srimadbhagawad.

His name was Sri KRISHNA because his complexion was dark (krishna means black). When he got the title of Maharshi, using his powers of meditation, he divided the Vedas into four; thus he was called Vedavyas or Vyasdeva. He was born on an island (dwip), so he was called Dwaipayan.

His mother was Satyavati and his father was Parashar. His grandfather was Shakti, the son of Vashishtha, the family priest of Rama.

He was born to Satyavati when she was single. When Vichitravirya died very young, by his mother's instructions he gave birth to Dhritarashtra from Ambika's womb, Pandu from Ambalika's womb and Vidura from a maid's womb.

He was very dark, had matted hair and looked fierce. On seeing him, Ambika had closed her eyes in fear. Thus Dhritarashtra, born of the union of Ambika and Vyasdeva, was born blind. Ambalika went pale with fright when she saw him; thus Pandu, born of the union between Ambalika and Vyasdeva, was born pale.

He had given Sanjay divine sight to be able to see the Kurukshetra and narrate it to Dhritarashtra. By his blessings, Dhritarashtra was able to see everybody after the war.

Vyasdeva's greatest creation, the *Mahabharata*, written in one hundred thousand slokas, is the greatest and longest epic of all time. The Srimadbhagawad section within the *Mahabharata* is considered the best.

Vyasdeva will be remembered forever for writing the *Mahabharata*. For this reason alone is he counted amongst the ten immortals.

Yadu

Son of YAYATI and DEVYANI. The famous Yadu dynasty started with him; the successors of this dynasty were called Yadavas. Krishna, Balarama and Subhadra were born of this lineage.

Yatugriha

A house constructed with inflammable materials like wax, flax, oil, wood and jute. DURYODHANA had such a house constructed in Varanavat in order to burn the PANDAVAS alive. VIDURA sent a digger to warn YUDHISHTHIRA. The Pandavas were saved.

BHEEMA set fire to Yatugriha and escaped through the tunnel that the digger had made. A hunter's wife was resting in the house of wax with her five sons. All six of them were burnt. Duryodhana assumed that KUNTI and the five Pandavas were killed. They pretended to be sorry but were actually glad.

Yashoda

KRISHNA's adopted mother and wife of NANDA. She was a devotee of Krishna. Yogmaya was born to her and in Kansa's prison cell Krishna was born to Devaki on the same night. Following divine orders, Vasudeva exchanged the two children. She brought up Krishna and Balarama with great affection.

Yagnaseni

Another name for DRAUPADI.

Yayati

Husband of DEVYANI, daughter of SUKRACHARYA and his wife Uryaswati. Since Yayati also married SARMISTHA, Sukracharya cursed him whereby Yayati aged prematurely. Sukracharya had also added a clause whereby Yayati could exchange his old age for another person's youth. But no one wanted this exchange.

Finally his son Puru agreed to the switch. Yayati took his son's youth and enjoyed sensual pleasures for another thousand years. Then he realized that true peace came from sacrifice and not from indulgence. He returned his son's youth to him and crowned him king. Then he performed severe meditation and went to heaven.

For more, see DEVYANI and SARMISTHA.

Yodheya

YUDHISHTHIRA's son by DEVIKA. He was killed by ASHWATHAMA in the war.

Yogmaya

NANDA's daughter, born of YASHODA. VASUDEVA exchanged her with KRISHNA. When KANSA, mistaking her for Devaki's daughter, picked her up to crush her to death, she slipped out of his hands and rose into the air. She said, 'The person who will kill you is being reared at Gokula.'

Yojangandha

Another name for SATYAVATI.

Yudhamanyu

A valiant warrior of Panchal. He was on the side of the PANDAVAS in the KURUKSHETRA.

Yudhishthira

Son of KUNTI and PANDU, though born of another. Dharma was his biological father. He always spoke the truth. He was calm, steady and steadfast to his principles. He told a lie or half-truths only twice. Once, during their stay in disguise he told King Virata that he was Yudhishthira's courtier Kanka; the other time that he told a half-truth was during the killing of Drona. He said, 'ASHWATHAMA has been killed' loudly and then whispered 'the elephant.'

Since he was the oldest amongst the PANDAVAS and the KAURAVAS, he was crowned successor to the throne. Duryodhana, blinded by jealousy, wanted to torch the Pandavas in a house of wax.

Yudhishthira lost everything twice by trickery in a game of dice. He personally witnessed Draupadi's humiliation. Yet he was willing to settle for just five villages in the hope that he could avert a war which would involve the killing of thousands of people.

He rescued Bheema from Nahush who, in the form of a snake, asked him complicated questions. Nahush, too, was relieved of his curse.

When Jayadratha abducted Draupadi, he forgave him, thinking of the plight of his cousin Dushala.

Yudhishthira had an interesting conversation with a crane who was actually Dharma in disguise. Yudhishthira's knowledge and wisdom were apparent in these conversations.

Just before the war commenced, Yudhishthira got down from his chariot and asked for the blessings of Bhishma, Drona, Kripacharya, Shalya and the others. This humility and sense of virtue becomes Yudhishthira.

Defeated by Karna, he returned from the battlefield and asked Arjuna to give up his Gandeev. Arjuna rushed to attack him. Realizing his own mistake, Yudhishthira was repentant.

When he went to pay his respects to Gandhari after the war, her angry, searing looks pierced the blindfold and fell on Yudhishthira's nails which became discoloured. He heard the Bhishma Gita from Bhishma for thirty days while the latter lay on his bed of arrows.

Yudhishthira ruled for thirty-six years; after that he handed over the reigns of the kingdom to Parikshit and went on his final journey with Draupadi and his brothers. Dharma, in the guise of a dog, followed them. One by one, Draupadi and the four brothers fell.

Indra brought a chariot to escort Yudhishthira. Yudhishthira insisted that he wanted to take the dog. After much discussion and argument, Dharma revealed his true form and blessed Yudhishthira. Yudhishthira went to heaven with his body intact.

He was surprised not to find his brothers there. Later, he was taken to an illusory hell, because of his lie about Ashwathama's death, and brought back to heaven where he met his brothers.

Yudhishthira had two wives: Draupadi and Devika. His son by Draupadi was called Prativindhya and his son by Devika was called Yodheya.

Yudhishthira spent about one hundred and nine years on earth. During his year in disguise, although he told everyone that his name was Kanka, his code name amongst the brothers was Jay.

Yuyutsu

DHRITARASHTRA's son, born of the Vaishya maid SAUBALI. He was younger than DURYODHANA and older than DUSHASANA.

During the KURUKSHETRA, one hundred sons of GANDHARI were killed by Bheema. Only Yuyutsu was alive. The virtuous YUYUTSU had responded to Yudhishthira's call and joined the PANDAVAS.

When Yudhishthira became king, Yuyutsu was a courtier. When the Pandavas left on their final journey, Yudhishthira made Parikshit the king and handed over the reigns to Yuyutsu.

When Gandhari was pregnant the maid Saubali had taken care of Dhritarashtra. It was then that she became pregnant and Yuyutsu was born.

Yuyutsu means one who is willing to fight; but this Yuyutsu was neither very aggressive in war nor very good at fighting.

Mythical Names of Some Places and their Present Names and Locations

When we read the *Ramayana* and the *Mahabharata* or other mythological stories we want to know the present location of places named and described in these stories. Where can we actually see these rivers, places, mountains and forests? To respond to readers' queries this section has been compiled. This list is incomplete but can satisfy the reader's curiosity to some extent.

Mythological name	Present name and location
Ahalyasrama or Gautamasrama	Jarail parganas, Trihut, 24 miles south-west of Janakpur
Amarkantak	Gondwana mountains, Nagpur (Mekal/Som/Amrakut Mountain)
Anga	Munger and Bhagalpur in Bihar
Andhra	North Tamil Nadu and part of Hyderabad
Asruk	An area in southern India
Avanti	Malav; Ujjaini, Madhya Pradesh
Ayodhya	Ayodhya, District Faizabad
Banga	Bangladesh
Batsya	An area west of Prayag and north of Yamuna
Badrikasrama (Naranarayanasrama)	An area in Kashmir
Bhoja	An area near Malav and Vidarbha or Bhopal
Brahmarshi	An area between the rivers Ganga and

	Yamuna, from Haridwar to Chambal and Kurukshetra near Delhi
Brahmavarta	Area between rivers Saraswati and Drishadwati
Charmanwati river	Chambal river
Chedi	Near Jabalpur, an area between the rivers Narmada and Godavari.
Chola	The area on the banks of the river Cauvery
Dandakaranya	Dandakaranya, Madhya Pradesh
Darad	Dardisthan, near Kashmir
Dasharna	An area between the rivers Chambal and Betwa in Madhya Pradesh
Dravid	South-east India
Dwaita forest	Deoband, on the banks of the river Saraswati in Punjab; Sahranpur
Ekchakra	Ara in Bihar (there are other opinions about the location of Ekchakra)
Falgu	The twin waters of Nilanjana and Mohana in Bihar
Gandhamadan mountains	North of the Rudra Himalayas; in Kailash, according to the Puranas
Gandhar	The area bordering Sind and Kabul rivers, the North-West Frontier Province
Giribraja	Rajgir in Bihar
Gautami	Godavari river
Gautamasrama	Another name for Ahalyasrama. See AHALYASRAMA
Hastinapur	East of Delhi; area on the south bank of the Ganga near Meerut
Indraprastha	City on the banks of the Yamuna, near old Delhi
Jansthan	Aurangabad; the land between the Godavari and Krishna rivers
Kalinga	The area along the Bay of Bengal, between the rivers Mahanadi and Godavari.
Kamboj	North Kashmir
Kamyak Forest	Near the Gulf of Kutch, the area along the river Saraswati
Kishkindhya	District of Bellary, south of the Tungabhadra; near Vijaynagar, close to Lake Pampa in Karnataka and Andhra Pradesh
Kekay	The area between the rivers Satadru and Bipasha (north-west of the river Indus,

	probably in the district of Shapur)
Keral	South-west India, Malabar and Karnataka and present-day Kerala
Kailash	Kailash. The Himalayan peak north-west of Manasarovar in Tibet.
Kaushiki river	River Kosi or Kesi
Khandavdaha	Indraprastha, near Delhi
Kosal	In Uttar Pradesh, near Ayodhya, Districts of Faizabad, Ganga and Bareich
Kosal (North)	North of this area
Kosal (South)	Chhattisgarh
Kuru (North)	North-west Tibet; according to some it is in Siberia
Kurukshetra	Districts of Ambala and Karnal in Punjab
Kurujangal	Kurukshetra and north of it
Lanka	Sri Lanka
Magadha	Area near Patna and Gaya.
Manipur	Not modern Manipur; the location of Manipur of the *Mahabharata* has not been identified.
Matsya	Rajputana; west of Dholpur or Jaipur
Madra	Punjab; the area between Chandrabhaga and Irawati.
Madhyadesh	The area between the Himalayas and Vindhya mountains, west of Prayag and east of Kurukshetra
Mandar mountains	Bhagalpur, Bihar
Mahendra mountains	Eastern Ghats
Malav	Malwa, Central India
Mahismati puri	District of Nimar on the banks of the Narmada, Madhya Pradesh
Mekal	Amarkantak, near the source of the river Narmada
Meru	Probably the Hindu Kush mountains
Mithila	Districts of Muzaffarpur and Darbhanga, Bihar
Naimisharanya	Nimkharvan or Nimsar; Sitapur in Uttar Pradesh
Nishedh	East of Jabalpur, Madhya Pradesh or in Kumaon, Uttaranchal
Oghavati	A tributary of the river Chitrabh, Apga
Panchvati	Nasik; on the banks of the Godavari river
Panchal	The area between the rivers Ganga and Yamuna, from Haridwar to Chambal
Paniprastha	Panipat, near Delhi

Pandya	Madura and Tinevelli in Tamilnadu
Pundru	North Bengal
Pradyumnanagar	Pandua, Hooghly, West Bengal
Pravas	A holy place in Kathiawad, by the sea; Pavosa
Pragjyotish	Kamrup, Assam
Prachya	An area east of the river Saraswati
Rishyamuk mountain	The mountain range between the Eastern Ghats and the Nilgiris, the source of Lake Pampa and river Cauvery
Raibatak mountains	Kathiawad, Girnar
Shalva	Area in Rajputana
Samantapanchak	Area with five lakes in Kurukshetra
Saurashtra	Kathiawad, Gujarat
Sumeru	Probably the Hindu Kush mountains
Sumha	Near Tamluk, Midnapore in West Bengal
Souvir	South of Rajputana or the Indus valley
Sage Kanva's ashram	Near Rajputana, on the banks of the river Malini
Takshasila	District of Rawalpindi, North-West Frontier Province
Trigarta	Kangra valley in Punjab's Jullundhur District (or the desert east of the river Satadru; according to some opinions, Lahore or Tahore)
Upaplavya	A city in the kingdom of Matsya, Rajputana. According to some, it is Jaipur in Rajasthan.
Varanavat	Varnawa; nineteen miles north-west of Meerut
Valmiki ashram	Vithur; fourteen miles north-west of Kanpur in Uttar Pradesh.
Vahik, Vahlik	Indus area or in Balakh area
Vidarbha	Berar
Videha	Mithila in North Bihar
Viswamitra ashram	Vedgarvapuri
Vrigu	Bagraseni; Baliya in Uttar Pradesh

Other Interesting Mythological Concepts

Readers sometimes have to struggle with complex words while reading the *Ramayana* and the *Mahabharata* and have to leaf through many books to find the meanings. Keeping this in mind, I have compiled these facts to save the reader the trouble.

My abilities are limited. Many of these facts have multiple interpretations. Wherever it has been possible, I have tried to represent plural perspectives.

1 manwantar

1 manwantar = Reign of Manu = 30,67,20,000 years

(Three hundred and six million, seven hundred and twenty thousand years)

There are fourteen manus. Each of them have reigned for 1 manwantar.

1 kalpa

1 kalpa = One day of Brahma's
= Reign of 14 manus
= 14x30,67,20,000 years

Theory of one God

The philosophy that there is only one God

Theory of two Gods

According to this philosophy, God has two forms, physical and spiritual or man and nature.

Dwairath

The fight between two warriors on chariots.

Trikaal

Past, present and future

The three families or lineages

The father's family, the mother's family and the in-laws' family

The three natural qualities

Goodness, spirit, ignorance

The three afflictions

Spiritual, material and supernatural

The three humours

Air, bile, phlegm

The three streams

Ganga's path in heaven, earth and the underworld:
    Heaven—Mandakini,
    Earth—Bhagirathi or Alaknanda,
    Underworld—Bhagwati

The three sins

The mortal sin, the punishable sin, the venial sin

The three holy fruit

Black myrobalan, emblica myrobalan, beleric myrobalan

The three pursuits of human life

Religion, wealth and love

Triveni

The place where the rivers Ganga, Yamuna and Saraswati meet

Trimurti

Brahma, Vishnu and Maheswar

The three jewels

Buddha, dharma, sangha

The three worlds

Heaven, earth and the underworld

The three parts of one day

Morning, midday and afternoon

The three syllables

A+u+m; this mantra

The four parts of an army

Elephant-riders, cavalry, charioteers and infantry

The four stages of human life

Brahmacharya or monastic and student life, grihastya or a householder's life, vanprastha or retired life and sanyasa or the life of an ascetic

The four pursuits of human life

Religion, wealth, love and salvation

The four castes

Brahmins, Kshatriyas, Vaishyas and Sudras

The four Vedas

Rig, Yaju, Sama and Atharva

Chatuspathi

A school where the four Vedas were taught or a school which teaches the four subjects: grammar, poetry, law and philosophy

The four Dasharathis

Rama, Lakshmana, Bharat and Shatrughna; Dasharth's four sons were called Dasharathis

The four saints

Sanak, Sanandan, Sanatkumar, Sanatan

The four eras (yugas)

Satya, Treta, Dwapar and Kali

The five daughters (panchkanya)

Ahalya, Draupadi, Kunti, Tara and Mandodari

The five Gangas

Bhagirathi, Gautami, Krishnaveni, Pinakini, Cauvery

The five articles derived from the cow

Yogurt, milk, clarified butter, urine and cowdung

Panchtapa

One who practises severe penance, with the sun overhead and four huge fires on either side. Sri Sri Ma Sarada Devi achieved salvation with this penance that she performed in Belur Math.

Panchtirtha

Kurukshetra, Gaya, Ganga, Pravas, Pushkar

The five deities who receive oblations before a meal

Ganesh, Gouri, Aditya, Rudra and Keshav

The five rivers of the Punjab, the land of five rivers

Satadru, Bipasha, Irawati, Chandrabhaga, Bitasta
Or
Pilgrimages on the banks of the five rivers: Kirana, Dhutapapa, Saraswati, Ganga, Yamuna

The five trees (panchvati)

Mango, peepul, banyan, fig and large fig trees

The five Pandavas

Yudhishthira, Bheema, Arjuna, Nakula and Sahadeva

The five fathers

The birth father, one who drives away fear, father-in-law, teacher and one who provides a job

The five trees in the forest

Peepul, banyan, wood apple, myrobalan, ashoka

The five vital elements

Earth, water, fire, air and atmosphere

The five essential ingredients to tantrik rites (pancha makara)

Wine (madira), meat (mamsa), fish (matsya), stance (mudra) and sexual intercourse (maithuna)

The five mortal sins

Slaying a Brahmin, robbing the property of a Brahmin, trying to obtain your teacher's wife, drinking alcohol and living in close proximity of people who are guilty of such sins

The five maha yagnas

Brahmin yagna, yagna for father, for gods, for vital elements and for man

The five gems

Sapphire, diamond, ruby, pearl and coral

The five parts of Time

Creation, secondary creation, lineage, manwantar and dissolution; without these the Puranas are not complete.

The five principal grains

Paddy, kidney beans, barley, sesame and pigeon pea

The five amrits

Milk, yogurt, clarified butter, honey and sugar

The five senses

(1) Senses of enlightenment: eyes, ears, nose, tongue, skin
(2) Functional senses: speech, hand, feet, anus, genitalia

The five implements of battle

Sword, bow and arrow, axe, armour, and without weapons

The five ingredients of rituals

Fragrance, flowers, incense, lamp, food

The six actions of a Brahmin

Worship, conducting religious ceremony for others, studying, teaching, charity and accepting gifts

The six parts of the body

Head, torso, two hands, two feet

The six parts of the Vedas

Education, the Hindu scriptures, grammar, Vedic glossary, rhythm and metre, astrology

The six seasons

Summer, monsoon, autumn, late autumn, winter, spring

The six systems of Hindu philosophy

Sankhya, Patanjal, Purbamimansa, Vedanta, Nyay, Vaishesik

The six juices

Salty, sour, dry, pungent, bitter, sweet

The six inherent sins of man (ripus)

Desire (kama), anger (krodh), greed (lobh), delusion (moha), arrogance (mada) and malice (matsarya)

The seven tongues (of fire)

(1) Kali, Karali, Manojaba, Sulohita, Sudhumravarna, Sphulingini, Vishwanirupini

The seven islands

Jambu, Kush, Plaksha, Shalmali, Crouncha, Shak, Pushkar

The kings of the seven islands

Agnidhra, Medhatithi, Bapushman, Jyotishman, Dyutiman, Bhavya, Saban

The seven levels of the underworld

Tal (ground level), atal (first level), vital, sutal, talatal, mahatal, rasatal (lowest level)

The seven winds

Bring in, flow, carry away, blow in the opposite direction, blow upwards, set in motion, move

The seven charioteers

They were seven charioteers who killed the helpless Abhimanyu in the Kurukshetra war. The following are the various versions of their identities:

(1) Karna, Dushasana, Kripacharya, Duryodhana, Dronacharya, Ashwathama, Jayadratha
(2) Dronacharya, Karna, Kripacharya, Ashwathama, Shakuni, Duryodhana, Dushasana
(3) Dronacharya, Karna, Kripacharya, Ashwathama, Vrihaddal, Kritavarma, Dushasana's son

(4) Dronacharya, Karna, Kripacharya, Ashwathama, Shakuni, Jayadratha, Dushasana

The seven great sages of ancient India

Marichi, Atri, Pulaha, Pulastya, Krotu, Angira, Vrigu (who was, according to some opinions, Vashishtha).

They lived in the age of the first Manu, Swayambhu.

The seven great sages during the reign of the seventh Manu, Vaivasat

Atri, Vashishtha, Kashyap, Gautama, Bharadwaj, Viswamitra, Jamadagni

It is currently the era of Vaivasat Manu.

For all practical purposes, there are ninety-eight sages in this list. Every Manu had his own list of gods, Indra, great sages, etc. So there are 14x7=98 sages.

Even if there are similarities in the names of the great ancient sages, they are different people because every Manu would destroy creation at the end of his reign of 30,67,20,000 years.

At the present time there are two opinions regarding whether Vrigu was the sage or Vashishtha. According to the opinion of God himself, in the Gita, he seems more likely to have been Vrigu.

Wives of the seven great ancient sages

Saint	Wife
Marichi	Kala
Atri	Anusuya
Pulaha	Kshama
Pulastya	Habirvu
Krotu	Sannati
Angira	Sraddha
Vashishtha	Arundhati
Vrigu	(1) Puloma according to the *Ramayana*
	(2)Kshyati according to the *Vishnu Purana*

The seven heavens

Vu, Vubaha, Swa, Yana, Maha, Tapa, Satya

The seven seas (of myth)

Salt, sugar cane juice, alcohol, clarified butter, yogurt, milk and water

The seven books of the Sama Vedas

Rathantar, Vrihatsom, Vamdeva, Vairup, Pavman, Vairaj, Chandra-mash

The seven verses

Gayatri or Vedic metre of versification, ushnig, anustup or a metre for poetry, vrihati or large poems, lines, three-line rhymes, earthly metre

The eight manifestations of goddess Kali

Mangala, Vimala, Sarvamangala, Kali, Ratrikalika, Vikata, Kamakshya, Bhawani

The eight female forms

Tara, Ugra, Mahogra, Vajra (or Kala), Kali, Saraswati, Kameshwari, Chamunda

The eight guardian deities at the eight points of the earth

Indra, Vahni, Yama, Naireet, Varuna, Marut, Kuber, Ishan

The eight elephants

Airavat, Pundareek, Vaman, Kumud, Anjan, Pushpadanta, Sarvabhouma, Suprateek

The eight virtues

Truth, purity, mercy, freedom from envy, forgiveness, kindness, generosity, happiness

The eight metals

Gold, silver, copper, bronze, bell metal, zinc, lead, iron

The eight chief snakes

Anant, Vasuki, Padma, Maha Padma, Takshak, Kulir, Karkat, Sankhya

The eight manifestations of Durga

Mangala, Vijaya, Bhadra, Jayanti, Aparajita, Nandini, Narsinghi, Koumari

The eight minor goddesses

Ugrachanda, Prachanda, Chandogra, Chandnayika, Atichanda, Chamunda, Chanda, Chandavati

The eight moods

Going to meet her lover, expecting her lover to come to her bed chamber, worried about her lover's absence, deceived by her lover, stricken with anger and jealousy on finding signs on her lover of him having visited another woman, feeling miserable for having quarrelled with and sent back her lover, enjoying control over the lover and separated from her lover as he has gone abroad

The eight binds

Hatred, insult, shame, prestige, temptation, pride, resentment, scandal mongering

The eight infallible weapons of the eight principal gods

The weapons of the eight gods and goddesses are together called the eight thunders.

Name of the God	Name of the Thunder
Vishnu	Sudarshan Chakra
Shiva	Trident
Brahma	Dice
Indra	Thunder
Varuna	Lasso
Yama	Rod
Kartik	Power
Durga	Sword

The eight Vasus

They are the eight sons of Dharma born of Daksha's daughter Vasu. There are many opinions regarding their names:

(1) Aap, Dhruv, Som, Dhar, Anil, Anal, Pratyush, Pravas
(2) Dhar, Dhruv, Som, Savitra, Anil, Anal, Pratyush, Pravas
(3) According to the *Vishnu Purana*—Drona (he is not Arjuna's teacher), Pran, Dhruv, Arka, Agni, Dosh, Vastu, Vibhabasu
(4) According to the *Mahabharata*—Bahurup, Trambak, Savitra, Dyu, Sureshwar, Jayant, Pinaki, Aparajita
(5) Bhav, Dhruv, Som, Vishnu, Anil, Anal, Pratyush, Pravabh
(6) Aap, Dhruv, Som, Anil, Anal, Dhar, Pratyush, Pravabh

The eight terrible manifestations of Shiva

Asitanga, Ruru, Chanda, Krodhonmatta, Bhayankar, Kapali, Bheeshan, Sanhar

The eight good omens

(1) Brahmin, cow, fire, gold, clarified butter, sun, water, king
(2) Lion, ram, elephant, aquarius, fan, chariot, conch shell, lamp
(3) A horse which has white marks on its four hooves, tail, mouth, chest and back

The eight manifestations

(1) Shiva's eight forms: Sarva, Bhava, Rudra, Ugra, Bheema, Pashupati, Mahadeva, Ishan

(2) The five vital elements, the sun, the moon, and one on whose behalf the priest worships

The eight companions of the goddess Durga

Sailaputri, Chandghanta, Skandamata, Kalratri, Chandika, Kushmandi, Katyani, Mahagouri

The eight superhuman qualities attainable by ascetic practise

Power, divine grace, pride, yogic attainment that enables one to make one's body lighter, attainment, ascetical power of moving or enjoying at will, godliness, perfect continence.

The eight parts of the body

(1) Two hands, heart, forehead, two eyes, voice, spine
(2) Two toes, two knees, two hands, chest, nose
(3) Restraint, discipline, seat, exercise, meditation, thought, trance

The nine emotions

Shringar (love), hasya (laughter), adbhuta (wonder), veera (courage), shanta (peace), karuna (sadness), rudra (anger), bhayanak (terrible), vibhatsa (disgust)

The nine grahas which represent the nine planetary principles of energy

Surya (Sun), Chandra (Moon), Mangala (Mars), Budha (Mercury), Brihaspati (Jupiter), Shukra (Venus), Shani (Saturn), Rahu and Ketu.

The nine manifestations of goddess Durga

(1) Parvati, Brahmacharini, Chandraghanta, Kushmanda, Skandamata, Katyani, Kalratri, Mahagouri, Siddhida
(2) Kali, Katyani, Ishani, Mundamardini, Chamunda, Bhadrakali, Bhadra, Twarita, Vaishnavi

The nine doors

Two eyes, two ears, the two nostrils, mouth, anus, genitals

The nine metals

Gold, silver, bronze, lead, copper, zinc, iron, bell metal, steel

The nine leaves

A female form made out of nine kinds of leaves, including plantain, colacacia, paddy, turmeric, pomegranate, wood apple, ashoka, jayanti and arum

The nine precious gems

Pearl, ruby, cat's eye, zircon, diamond, red coral, beryl, emerald and sapphire.

The court of King Vikramaditya also had nine gems or famous people including Dhanwantari, Khapanak, Amarsinha, Sanku, Betalbhatta, Ghatkarpar, Kalidas, Varahamihira, Vararuchi.

The nine attributes of purity

Courtesy, humility, learning, success, pilgrimage, sincerity, profession, ascetic practices, charity

The nine forces

Vimala, utkarshani, gyana, yoga, kriya, prahari, Satya, ishnai, Anugra

The nine communities

The spice dealer, the garland maker, the weaver, the milkman, the barber, one who grows betel leaves, the blacksmith, the potter and the sweet-maker

The ten Hindu sacraments

Pregnancy, sacrament performed in the third month of pregnancy to have a male child, sacrament received by a pregnant woman, rites to be performed at birth, naming ceremony, feeding the first rice, shaving the head while leaving a tuft of hair uncut, sacred thread ceremony, convocation, marriage

The ten immortals

Vishnu, Kak, Markandeya, Ashwathama, Bali, Vyasa, Hanuman, Vibhishana, Kripa, Parasurama

The ten directions

Mythological Name	Modern Name
Purva	East
Agni	South-east
Dakshin	South
Naireet	South-west
Paschim	West
Vayu	North-west
Uttar	North
Ishan	North-east
Urdhwa	Above
Adha	Below

The ten protectors of the ten directions

Direction	God/protector
East	Indra
Agni	Agni
South	Yama
South-west	Nireet
West	Varuna
North-west	Marut
North	Kuber
Ishan	Ish
Above	Brahma
Below	Anant

The ten positives

Charity, conduct, forgiveness, virility, meditation, yagna, power, resource, concentration, enlightenment

The ten manifestations of goddess Durga

Kali, Tara, Sorashi, Bhuvaneshwari, Vairabhi, Chinnamasta, Dhumavati, Bagala, Matangi, Kamala (or Rajrajeswari).

The ten sins that can be washed away

On the tenth day of the month of Jaishtha during the waxing moon is the day when Ganga came to earth. If on that day one bathes in the river Ganga then all the following ten sins can be washed away:

1. Stealing
2. Killing animals forbidden in the Shastras
3. Sexual union with another man's wife
4. Violent behaviour
5. Telling untruths
6. Cruelty
7. Giving misleading information
8. Envy of other's possessions
9. Wanting to harm others
10. Fraud

The first four are physical sins, the next three are sins of speech and the last three are sins of thought.

The ten phases of the human mind

Motivation, thought, memory, adoration, worry, delirium, madness, illness, infirmity, death

The ten avatars

Matsya, Kurma, Varaha, Narasimha, Vaman, Parasurama, Rama, Krishna, Buddha, Kalki

The ten kinds of sons

Born biologically, born of another man, adopted, born through artificial means, born through the anus, illegitimate, born when the mother is single, born when the mother was pregnant during mariage, son belonging to a widowed wife from a previous marriage, a child that is purchased, the son of a man by a Sudra woman.

The eleven physical forms

Aja, Ekpad, Ahibrandha, Pinaki, Aparajita, Ambak, Makeswar, Vrishakapi, Sambhu, Haran, Ishwar

The twelve suns

They were born to Aditi and Kashyap. They are Dhata, Mitra, Aryama, Rudra, Varuna, Surya, Bhag, Bibaswan, Pusha, Savita, Twasta, Vishnu
    According to other versions they are Bibaswan, Aryama, Dhata, Mitra, Rudra, Varuna, Bhag, Pusha, Savita, Twasta, Vishnu, Urukram

The twelve months

Vaisakh, Jaishtha, Ashar, Sravan, Bhadra, Ashwin, Kartik, Agrahayan, Poush, Magh, Phalgun, Chaitra

The twelve signs of the zodiac

Mesh, Vrisha, Mithuna, Karkata, Simha, Kanya, Tula, Vrishchika, Dhanu, Makara, Kumbha, Meen

The twelve letters

The twelve letters of the Sanskrit alphabet contained in the mantra 'Om nama bhagawate vasudevaya'.

The fourteen lessons

The six Vedangas, the four Vedas, mimansa, law, history and the Puranas

The fourteen worlds

The seven heavens and the seven underworlds

The fourteen Manus

1. Swayambhuv, Swarochish, Uttam, Tamas, Raibat, Chakhush, Vaivasat, Sabarni, Dakshasabarni, Brahmasabarni, Rudra Sabarni, Dharmasabarni, Devsavarni, Indrasavarni
2. According to the *Matsya Purana*, Swayambhuv, Swarochish, Uttam, Tamas, Raibat, Chakhush, Vaivasat, Sabarni, Rochya, Bhoutya, Meru Sabarni, Ribhu, Ritubhama, Bishkaksen

The sixteen female deities

Gouri, Padma, Sachi, Medha, Savitri, Vijaya, Jaya, Devsena, Swadha, Swaha, Santi, Pusti, Dhriti, Tushti, the God of the family, One's own God

The sixteen things that can be given away in charity

Land, seat, water, clothes, lamp, rice, betel leaf, umbrella, fragrance, garlands, fruit, bedding, footwear, cow, gold, silver

The sixteen articles given in offering or used in worship

1. For the worship of Shakti: footwear, gifts, something to wash your hands with, ablutions, clothes, jewellery, fragrance, flowers, incense sticks, food, washing of hands and mouth of the God, spirits, betel leaf, using water to offer prayer to a departed soul, genuflection.
2. For worship of other kinds: mat to sit on, welcome, footwear, gifts, something to wash the hand with, something to wash the hand and face with after eating, an oblation of honey, clarified butter, milk, yogurt and sugar, bathing, clothes, ornaments, fragrance, flowers, incense sticks, lamp, food, sandalwood paste

The eighteen Maha Puranas

Vishnu, Naradiya, Bhagawat, Garura, Padma, Varaha, Brahma, Brahmanda, Brahmavaivarta, Markandeya, Bhavisya, Baman, Matsya, Kurma, Linga, Shiva, Skanda, Agni

The first six of these have the quality of goodness, the next six deal with the spirit and the last six are about ignorance.

The eighteen Upapuranas

Sanatkumar, Narasimha, Naradiya, Shiva, Durvasa, Kapil, Manav, Oushanas, Varuna, Kalika, Shamba, Nandy, Soura, Parashar, Aditya, Maheswar, Bhagawat, Vashishtha

The eighteen modes of learning

The four Vedas, education, Kalpa, grammar, Vedic glossary, metre, astrology, Mimansa, law, Dharmashastras, Puranas, Ayurveda, Dhanurved, gandharva, Arthshastra

The twenty-seven stars or the moon's twenty-seven wives

Aswini, Bharani, Kristina, Rohini, Mrigashira, Ardra, Punarvasu, Pushya, Ashlesha, Magha, Purvaphalguni, Uttarphalguni, Hasta, Chitra, Swati, Visakha, Anuradha, Jestha, Mula, Purvashara, Uttarashara, Sravana, Dhanistha, Satabhisha, Purvabhadrapadi, Uttarbhadrapadi, Revati.

More Facts

How long did each era last?

Era	Number of Years
Satya	17,28,000 years (four times of Kaliyuga)
Treta	12,96,000 years (three times of Kaliyuga)
Dwapar	8,64,000 years (twice Kaliyuga)
Kali	4,32,000 years

What were Jay and Vijay in their various births?

Name	Yuga		
	Satya	Treta	Dwapar
Jay	Hiranakshya	Ravana	Sisupala
Vijay	Hiranyakashipu	Kumbhkarna	Dantabakra

About the Vedas

The Vedas are the main texts for the Hindus that set the right path and the tenets of morality. The unwritten Vedas have come down the ages in the form of Srutis. Saints are said to have heard the Vedas from Brahma himself. The scope of the Vedas have widened gradually.

Vyasdeva divided the Vedas into four: the *Rig Veda, Sama Veda, Yajur Veda* and *Atharva Veda*. Thus he was called Vedavyas. Sometimes the *Mahabharata* is called the fifth Veda. The four Vedas have some science-based subtexts. They are:

Veda	Subtext
Rig	Ayurveda
Sama	Gandharvaveda
Yajur	Dhanurveda
Atharva	Sthapatyaveda

Vedangas—To understand the Vedas better there are six sections that are part of the Vedas. They are learning, scriptures, grammar, metre, astrology and a Vedic glossary.

Vedanta and Upanishad—the concluding part of the Vedas are called Vedanta or Upanishad. The essence of the Vedas are contained in these.

Philosophy

Hindu philosophy has six sections. They are:

Philosophy	Composer
Sankhya	Kapil
Yoga	Patanjal
Vaishesik	Kanad
Nyay	Gautama
Mimansa	Jaimini
Vedanta	Vyasdeva

About the Puranas

The various discourses of the saints and sages regarding society, religion, science, and the theory of Brahma are called the Puranas. With these have been connected many beautiful parables.

There are two kinds of Puranas: the Maha Puranas and Upapuranas. Each has eighteen sections. The Maha Puranas are also divided according to the primal quality of goodness, spirit and ignorance.

Puranas

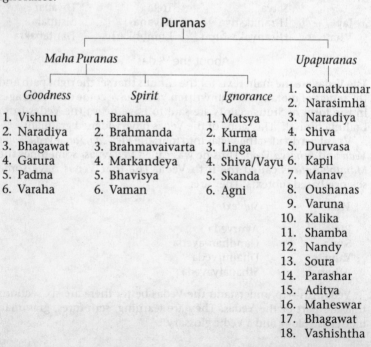

Maha Puranas

Goodness	Spirit	Ignorance
1. Vishnu	1. Brahma	1. Matsya
2. Naradiya	2. Brahmanda	2. Kurma
3. Bhagawat	3. Brahmavaivarta	3. Linga
4. Garura	4. Markandeya	4. Shiva/Vayu
5. Padma	5. Bhavisya	5. Skanda
6. Varaha	6. Vaman	6. Agni

Upapuranas

1. Sanatkumar
2. Narasimha
3. Naradiya
4. Shiva
5. Durvasa
6. Kapil
7. Manav
8. Oushanas
9. Varuna
10. Kalika
11. Shamba
12. Nandy
13. Soura
14. Parashar
15. Aditya
16. Maheswar
17. Bhagawat
18. Vashishtha